SHIELDS
OF BRASS

or

SHIELDS
OF GOLD?

REESTABLISHING A STANDARD OF EXCELLENCE
IN THE CHURCH OF THE LORD JESUS CHRIST

O. S. HAWKINS

Shields of Brass or Shields of Gold

© 1998 O. S. Hawkins

A Publication of the Annuity Board
of the Southern Baptist Convention

Printed in the United States of America
Presented Free as a Facilitating Ministry of the
Annuity Board of the Southern Baptist Convention, Dallas, Texas

Dedicated to
Dr. Jack Graham, Pastor of the Prestonwood Church in
Dallas

My lifelong friend who sticks closer than a brother.

In the late sixties we preached together in the streets and in the rescue missions of Fort Worth...In the seventies we pastored a few miles from one another in Oklahoma...In the eighties we pastored near one another in Florida....and in the nineties God brought us both back to Dallas to pastor in the same city with one another. Our lives have been woven together since our teenage years and our accountability relationship has challenged us to love the Lord, our families, our church and one another.

Like King David, Jack leads "With the integrity of his heart and the skillfulness of his hands" and is doing the best job of anyone I know in reaching our modern culture without compromising the principles of scripture.

Table of Contents

Introduction 5

Part One   Reestablishing a Standard of Excellence 7

Chapter 1   The Standard of Excellence Revealed 11

Chapter 2   The Standard of Excellence Removed 15

Chapter 3   The Standard of Excellence Replaced 21

Chapter 4   The Standard of Excellence Restored 31

Part Two   Change is not a Four Letter Word 33

Chapter 5   Option #1 Change Can Be Rejected 39

Chapter 6   Option #2 Change Can Be Respected 47

Part Three   Four Pillars of Biblical Church Growth 61

Chapter 7   Participation 65

Chapter 8   Proclamation 81

Chapter 9   Preservation 111

Chapter 10   Propagation 127

Part Four   The No Fear Culture 139

Chapter 11   A Why Question 143

Chapter 12   A What Question 149

Chapter 13   A How Question 157

Part Five   Engaging the Culture 161

Chapter 14   Discernment in Comprehending the Culture 167

Chapter 15   Direction in Confronting the Culture 175

Introduction

As the church of the Lord Jesus Christ enters and engages the new millennium we find ourselves in many ways like the Kingdom of Judah during the reign of King Rehoboam. Shishak of Egypt had invaded Israel and had stolen the three hundred shields of pure gold which King Solomon had made as a testimony to God and as a standard of excellence in his kingdom. Rehoboam was faced with two options. He could humble himself, stop lamenting about what might have been, and walk by faith and vision into a new day of victory. Or, he could continue to make things look on the surface as they did in the glory days of Solomon's kingdom. He chose the latter. He commissioned three hundred shields to be made of brass, cheap imitations, which needed constant polishing and human effort to make them look like gold.

As the church ministers in the twenty-first century, she too is often guilty of substituting shields of brass for shields of gold. This volume is a call to see the importance of reestablishing a standard of excellence to the New Testament pattern of church health and growth. It also delineates the changes needed to establish that standard and outlines the way to not simply speak to a modern culture, but to engage and convert it.

Southern Baptists are a diverse people. We are the true "rainbow" denomination encompassing every race and color imaginable. We pride ourselves in having "no creed but the Bible." Thus we are diverse in our interpretations of such things as doctrines of grace and eschatology to simply name a couple of subjects. This volume is an appeal to the church for balance. Those churches who have grown stale, and have perhaps lost their sense of vision or their spirit of conquest, will find in these pages a challenge to allow the fresh wind of change to blow through their congregations. Those who worship at the altar of traditions that are simply cultural and not Biblical will find a challenge to break free. Those who, in their quest to become relevant to younger adult generations, have left Biblical, New Testament patterns of church growth and church health in their wake will be challenged to cease sacrificing revelation on the altar of relevancy. This is also a word to the modern church in a day when many who are "seeker sensitive" have forgotten that the real Seeker is the one with the capital "S." Balance is the key to reaching and discipling a twenty-first century world. These pages are intended to bring each of us to a time of examination and decision as to whether for us it will be...SHIELDS OF BRASS OR SHIELDS OF GOLD?

Part One

Reestablishing A Standard of Excellence

Aviation is fascinating. Isn't it amazing how a jet airliner as large as a football field, loaded with people and freight, can run down a concrete road and sail into the air with the greatest of ease? To look at this monstrosity sitting on a runway, you would not think it could move more than 5 miles per hour. I have flown in all sizes of airplanes. Each one of them has unique benefits and limitations. However, they all have the same purpose, and they all follow the same laws of aerodynamics.

Churches in many ways are like airplanes. Some resemble little Piper Cubs. They do not carry many passengers, but are easy to maneuver and operate. There are churches that resemble King Airs which are small but faster than the Piper Cubs.

Still other churches are like corporate jets. Luxurious and compact, they carry one kind of passenger–the business executive–to his destination fast.

Then, there are the B-52 bomber churches. They are old, out-of-date and sluggish and so they compensate by dropping bombs on everybody.

Of course, there are elegant and impressive 747 churches, so large they fit only a few places, but are instantly famous for their size alone.

In the Southern Baptist Convention we have a number of these 747 churches. Jumbo churches. There are passengers in first class and business class sections. The largest number of people sit in the coach section. There is a great diversity of ethnic, special needs groups and a broad list of ministries. These churches face the challenge every year to raise millions of dollars to continue these ministries.

Unfortunately, some 747 churches are losing speed, altitude and passengers. They need to change direction. A pilot knows that the jumbo jet cannot be turned on a dime. A 90-degree turn would result in a larger loss of altitude and air speed. Passengers would panic and scatter to the side of the turn making the plane off balance. Sudden changes can be frightening.

Uneasiness on the part of passengers (congregations) is not confined to mega-churches; it may be even more pronounced in small churches. In the majority of Southern Baptist churches, 50 upset members can result in a crash. In thousands of congregations, one upset family can bring down the flight!

A 747 is turned at a 30-degree angle. When it turns at the proper angle and speed, you hardly feel it. If you have ever ridden on one of those big jumbo jets, you hardly even know it's making an approach turn into an airport.

As we enter the twenty-first century, our churches—large and small—need to make some turns. In 2 Chronicles 12 the Kingdom of Israel was dividing. Israel had three kings–Saul, David and Solomon. Solomon's son Rehoboam had risen to the throne of the tribe of Judah in the southern kingdom.

Rehoboam was so wicked that God allowed the Egyptians to rob and trample the temple. Among the items stolen were the golden shields that God had instructed Solomon to make and place at the temple during worship. The golden shields represented God's standard of excellence.

Embarrassed by the Egyptian defeat, Rehoboam commissioned craftsmen to make 300 new shields from brass. Rehoboam knew the brass shields were a cheap imitation, but if these shields were polished every day, he could pass them off as the real thing.

The modern church needs to make an honest diagnosis now, and evaluate where we have substituted shields of brass for God's standard of excellence, shields of gold.

Once Rehoboam was robbed of the former glory, he was faced with two options. We are faced with the same two options in a day, when in many ways, the glory of the church has waned.

First, we can humble ourselves, admit it, come before God and repent. We need to stop lamenting about what might have been and begin walking again by faith with new hearts.

The other choice is that we can continue to try to make things appear on the surface as they once were. Like Rehoboam, we can hold up a cheap substitute before the world, but it will not bear close inspection; it will not stand the test of time. We can keep polishing brass to make it look like gold, but eventually, we will go the way of ancient Israel. Our influence and witness in the world will continue to fade to a mere shadow.

Chapter One

The Standard of
Excellence Revealed

The twenty-first century is full of promise, but many churches are like computer systems with a Millennium bug. They will wake up one day and find the programs do not work anymore. Before that day arrives, we must change our mind-sets, and reprogram the operating system. When we face some realities and set a course to engage with relevance a young culture, we will win them with the Gospel of Jesus Christ.

The glory of Solomon's kingdom is beyond description. There may never have been a building more impressive than the temple that Solomon built in Jerusalem. The glory of his kingdom was a sign of God's blessing and God's approval. God designed it all. God instructed how it should be built. In his early days, King Solomon loved the Lord and walked in the statutes of David his father. God blessed him. (1 Kings 3:3)

In 1 Kings 4:29ff.: God gave Solomon wisdom and exceedingly great understanding and largeness of heart like the sand of the seashore. Thus Solomon's wisdom excelled the wisdom of all the men of the East and all the wisdom of Egypt for he was wiser than all men and his fame was in all the surrounding nations. He wrote three thousand proverbs and his songs were one thousand and five. In 1 Kings 10, it says all the earth sought the wisdom of Solomon which

God had put in his heart. Solomon made 300 shields of gold. Each one of them contained approximately three pounds of solid gold (I Kings 10:17). Can you imagine that sight?

I stood on the temple mount in Jerusalem and tried to imagine the length of a football field lined on two sides with those armor-bearers holding the shields of gold reflecting the bright Middle Eastern sun as the king made his way up to the temple to worship. Some commentators say that the shields were large enough to hide the man holding them. All you would see was the golden shield.

Those golden shields symbolized the *purity*, *integrity* and the *glory* of Jehovah God and His blessings upon His people. They showed God's standard of excellence. These shields of gold were never meant to be used in war. They were only brought out of their vault when the king was going to the temple to worship. The guards would form a double line, holding those golden shields for the king to walk through them.

The shields were not Solomon's idea. All of the plans for the temple came from God himself. They were part of God's design. If we could see them, it would be as if the temple itself were holding out its open arms to welcome those who came to worship.

God has established a standard of excellence for his church. His standard of excellence is revealed in the Book of Acts and in the Epistles. Many churches have forsaken God's standard of excellence revealed in the scriptures by buying into slick market-driven public relations approaches advocated by modern church gurus. Many of these experts have never been pastor of a church. The Bible, not Madison Avenue, gives us a model. We have a pattern for excellence. We see it in the Jerusalem church. We see it in the Antiochan church. We see it in the Philippian church. We need to take these Biblical principles and interpret them into the language and actions that people today can understand. The size of the congregation is irrelevant. The standard of excellence fits all.

The early church engaged its culture—a pagan culture. They did not do it by holding fast to previous traditions of religion. Of course there were some people who did not want to change a thing. That's what the Jerusalem conference was about in Acts 15. Christians gathered in a conference and decided that they were not going to impose their Jewish religious traditions and cultural habits upon a new generation of people who were embracing the Gospel of Jesus Christ.

They applied the standard of excellence: prayer, dependence upon the Holy Spirit, the power of God working and yielding through them, as they engaged a culture. They did not care who got the glory. They worshipped. They equipped believers. They broke out of their shells. They went outside where the people were, out in the agora, out in the marketplace, and there they engaged their culture.

God has a standard of excellence. The Church of Jesus Christ desperately needs to rediscover that standard. If we do, the glory of God will come. If we do not, we will hobble into a new millennium substituting shields of brass for shields of gold, holding up cheap substitutes that only appear to be the real thing.

Chapter Two

The Standard of Excellence Removed

Shishak, the pharaoh of Egypt, attacked Israel (2 Chronicles 12), and stole the 300 shields of gold. The standard of excellence was removed from the people of God because they had forsaken Him.

In verse 5, God said that because you have forsaken me, you will fall. They were invaded from the outside because they became infected from the inside. They forgot God. They forgot that God is a sovereign Lord.

We find this warning over and over in Scripture. Before the children of Israel went into the promised land, Moses, who was about to die on Mount Nebo, preached to his people not to forget and forsake God. In Deuteronomy 11, Moses warned the Israelites about turning to idolatry and the results that would come from their sin. The Israelites abandoned God and there was a drought.

After Rehoboam rose to power and established the kingdom of Judah, he forgot God. The Bible says God left him. The glory, the standard of excellence, was removed.

At the end of Solomon's reign his glory waned and greatness wilted. His kingdom was divided. Enemies hovered around Jerusalem. Five years into the reign of Rehoboam, Shishak of Egypt robbed Israel of her former glory. Rehoboam ignored God's law; he abandoned God's standards. There are a lot of churches who stood and watched their former greatness wane and wilt and their own kingdoms divide for the same reasons. Now they are still polishing brass. They are still trying to shine up the outside to make it look as if nothing has changed.

There is a famous American church that has deep roots in the Confederacy. It has a large endowment fund. When that fund was created during the first generation after the Civil War, its formal, legal purpose was to ensure that the building would be preserved as a historic landmark should it ever cease to be a church. No statement of purpose about witness or ministry; just be sure the brass is polished and the roof does not leak!

Rehoboam inherited his kingdom from the great King Solomon who ended up drowning himself in his own kingdom and his own pride. He admitted his failures at the end. In Ecclesiastes, he said, *look, it's all vanity*. Rehoboam called in the consultants for advice on what he should say to the people. He spoke with the elders in 1 Kings 12 and asked "What are we going to do?" Their advice was sound. *"If you'll be a servant to them and serve them, and speak good words to them, they'll be your servants forever"* (1 Kings 12:7).

That was not good enough for Rehoboam. He consulted the young crowd who told him to disregard the advice of those old men. They said you get up there and you say to the people, look, my little finger will be thicker than my father's waist (1 Kings 12:10).

Contradictory counsel is still around. There is a tension in many churches. Some circles of younger church leaders are saying everything should center on man, not around God. It's called seeker-friendly. Design your services, they say, so as not to offend the seeker (lost person). That's good, except there is one thing we need to remember. *God is the Seeker, not us.* He not only came after us when we were not looking for him; he came after us when we were hiding from him.

Jesus said, "I came to *seek* and to save those who are lost." Instead of creating an atmosphere where an unsaved person can be comfortable, our job is to create an atmosphere where the *Seeker*—God himself—is comfortable. He needs to be comfortable in the praises of his people. The Psalmist (22:3) says that God *inhabits the praises of his people.* He is the *Seeker.*

There is a very subtle implication taking place in modern church growth. I was talking to a young preacher who boasted about how he never preached as he was taught in seminary anymore. He said that he disregards the context and exposition because the "seeker" does not want to hear a Bible message, so he says you have to make it relevant to fill the needs of their life.

Many Seeker-friendly churches tend to disregard doctrinal truth and controversial issues. They do not confront people with the fact that they must make a decision of what to do with Jesus Christ. So much modern church philosophy is geared to making sure the seeker (with a little "s") is not offended. He or she is the center of all processes of worship preparation. It all centers on people, and when this happens the *Seeker* is offended, but He is the true *Seeker.*

I recently received a direct mail promotion advertising a church in the Dallas-Fort Worth Metroplex. Across the top it says *"Top Ten Reasons to Avoid Church."* This is their appeal to try to get people into their church. It's a clever little piece. Here are some of the promises the church makes. *If you come to our church it will all be over in less than an hour and "you will still have plenty of time to enjoy the day."* That's the offer.

Can you imagine Jesus Christ saying, "Come give me just a little less than an hour and then you can go on and enjoy the rest of your day. You can do what you want to do"? *Shields of brass for shields of gold.*

The mail piece also promises to *not make you listen to a bunch of old songs and an organ.* Strange, since the Scripture itself says we're to praise him on the stringed instruments and organs. The early church did not have the New Testament. They had the Old Testament. The early church hymnal was the Psalms. They sang the Psalms– pretty old stuff. *Shields of brass for shields of gold.*

Here's another thing, another promise if you will come to that church. When you come to our church, *leave your wallet at home. We promise not to talk about money.* Strange, since the Bible says honor the Lord with the first fruits of all your increase. Can you imagine Jesus Christ saying, "Follow me, and keep your money and everything else to yourself." No, he said, "Where your treasure is, that's where your heart will be also." *Shields of brass for shields of gold.*

Here's another promise. *We promise not to visit you.* Strange, since the early church was going everywhere in the marketplace sharing the Gospel of Christ. The Lord Jesus would never say we promise not to confront you or to visit you. He said go out in the highways and the hedges and compel them to come. He said, "You shall receive power when the Holy Ghost has come upon you and you will be witnesses unto me in Jerusalem, Judea, Samaria, and everywhere to the ends of the earth." *Shields of brass for shields of gold.*

Here's another pledge. *You can blend in with our people and not be recognized.* Can you imagine Simon Peter saying that to the church in Jerusalem? Can you imagine Jesus Christ saying come to be a part of this church and you can blend right in and nobody will ever even know whether you are a believer or not? *Shields of brass for shields of gold.*

Here's one other one. *We will give you coffee and doughnuts free.* There are many churches today that do little or nothing to proclaim the death of Christ. It's seldom mentioned. There is no sign to proclaim the sacrificial work of God. Would to God we could invite Simon Peter to our churches and hear his commentary on this Seeker-friendly message. Peter was beaten, he was threatened to never speak the name of Jesus Christ again, and what did he do? He went away rejoicing that he was counted worthy to suffer for his name.

Would to God that we could invite Paul to our churches and put such a seeker message in his hand. Paul was stoned at Lystra; he was beaten in Philippi; he was martyred in Rome. Can you see him trying to build a church in Philippi with this promise—*We will give you free coffee and doughnuts?* Offering a brand of Christianity that entertains, that wants to meet the self-gratification needs of a yuppie culture without compelling anyone to bear a cross, is foreign to the New Testament Gospel. *Shields of brass for shields of gold.*

There is a tremendous truth in the need to be seeker-sensitive. We have an opportunity to bring balance. Much of the seeker sensitive methodology is out of balance. We need to engage our culture. There are people who have not been in church in years. Our verbiage and all of our ecclesiology are a foreign language to them. We should not abandon or water down the message. We need the pure gold of the Gospel.

There are churches everywhere that are disbanding because they are in transitional neighborhoods. Some of the leadership in some of those churches became locked in a time warp, and their church died. They kept saying we did it this way in the '50s and the '60s. That's why their churches died in the 90s. They never realized that a new culture has to be engaged where they are. We will never reach the cities of America unless we can develop a missionary mentality that people can relate to today.

The *Christian message never changes.* The methods do. Worship styles and people's needs change with the times, but many churches lag behind. We are the style setters.

What happened to churches over the last decade or so? Maybe we were too proud of wineskins that worked years ago. Maybe we wanted to thrive on the applause and the amen of men, and when that happens, God always allows Shishak to come. We blame our failures on Shishak or Smith or Jones or whomever, and that's why so many thousands of churches are dead. The glory has been removed.

Chapter Three

The Standard of Excellence Replaced

Have we lost our edge? Are we irrelevant? What happened to quality, not quantity? How do we reestablish a standard of excellence in today's church? I find that one of the challenges for churches as we go into a new millennium is, how do we find answers for these questions.

Remember your last trip to the mall. You walked by store after store, most selling clothes. Clothing is designed to cover your body, to keep you warm. What makes you walk into one of those stores? All of those vendors' products fulfill the primary purpose: to cover and to warm.

Have you ever stopped in one of those stores and thought you stepped back in time? There on the racks were things that a typical adult would not wear today. Instead, there were a lot of polyester double-knit suits on mannequins. You saw polyester leisure suits, some bright yellow and some pastel colors. Men in the shoe section had on these patent leather shoes that people were wearing in the 70s.

That store would appear to be locked in a time warp. They also would soon be having a going out of business sale. Down the corridor is some bright new store. There, you find clothes that are in style, that meet the needs of a changing culture. Meanwhile, the first store management wonders why people no longer like their consistency. Styles, fabrics and colors change. What sold years ago does not attract customers today.

There are many ways in which the church has been locked in a time warp. I noticed in one of the churches I pastored, that in our quest to build all of our ministries, our facility had been left unkept. Even though we had a wonderful product, many people never came because the disrepair and musty smell was a barrier. In unity, the church responded by building state-of-the-art nurseries and a children's building not to be found anywhere else. We wanted to produce a product there that men and women are going to be proud to wear in the coming days.

Rehoboam, David's grandson, inherited a powerful history. We read in 2 Chronicles 12 where Rehoboam ascended to the throne of Judah, the southern kingdom in a divided Israel. Rehoboam did not have a great start. Verse 1 tells us that Rehoboam did three things: established the kingdom, strengthened himself, and forsook the law of the Lord and all Israel along with him.

That can happen to a lot of people. It can happen to churches. We become established, we strengthen ourselves, so everything is going wonderfully well. If we are not careful, we lose sight of how we got there and who put us there. In the process, we forsake the law of the Lord. That's what Rehoboam did. He took all of Israel along with him.

God's standard of excellence was shown during Solomon's kingdom. Gold, which symbolizes purity and integrity, was a standard of excellence. The whole world looked upon Jerusalem. They were the superpower of their day in the height of Solomon's kingdom, and they gave to the world, the whole world, a true standard of excellence, and we saw the standard of excellence revealed.

When you consider your circumstances, ask yourself if you lost your standard of excellence? If we have lost the standard of excellence, why, and how? Perhaps pride–too proud of the past to change. Perhaps taking glory that belongs to God. Oh, we can blame our failures on Shishak and all sorts of other things. That's one reason there are thousands of churches empty. They are dying because, like Israel, we have rebelled against God. The standard of excellence has been removed.

Many of us have done the same thing Rehoboam did. We have replaced shields of gold with shields of brass. The shields probably worked fine. They may have even been good. The good instead of the best. Often, good is the enemy of the best. In (2 Chronicles 12:10) is one of the saddest verses in the Bible. It speaks of compromise. It speaks of cheaper substitution and imitation.

Have we done the same in our own personal lives, or in our church lives? Do we say things and do things, trying our best to make things look like a standard of excellence. When do we try to substitute what is good for what is best? You know, brass may look like gold for a little while. In fact, if you work real hard and put in a lot of effort, you can keep it polished where it will look almost like gold.

When we built a new auditorium in one of my former pastorates there was brass everywhere. It looked beautiful. Every time somebody touched it we had to spend a lot of time the next day polishing it again.

There is a difference between gold and brass. One is a pure metal; the other one is an alloy. Brass is made primarily of copper and zinc. One shines and the other dulls. One is tempered and strong and the other one is weak and cheap and a counterfeit.

At Pentecost the church began with the highest standards, shields of gold. We read in the early chapters of Acts the power of God and the glory of God on the early church. They engaged their pagan culture in virtually one generation, because they had a standard of excellence. Something began to take place as the centuries unfolded. Constantine embraced Christianity and joined it with the world. Throughout church history it's been a story of the church from time to time, from century after century, in various and sundry ways, substituting shields of brass for shields of gold. It's the same old game the enemy always plays. Substituting what is good for what is best. Some of us still fall for the same old trick.

Some of us live with brass relationships. Not long ago church people called everybody brother or sister so-and-so. We do not do that much anymore. When I was growing up, that was always strange to me. I came to the conclusion that people used this form of address to make up for the past. We really do not live like brothers and sisters. For example, if you had a brother, say his name was Bobby, you did not come to the breakfast table and say, oh, hello, Brother Bobby, how are you? No, you called him by his name. Why? Because you lived like brothers. Everybody knew you were brothers.

The church so often has brass relationships and we do not live like part of the family of God. From time to time we have to tag those names on, hoping that the lost world will at least see by our nomenclature that we are family.

We come before him with brass worship. Some of us bring brass gifts to him. The most prominent word in the Greek New Testament that we translate worship is a word that means to reverence or to bow. Literally, it means to kiss, to kiss toward. Do we leave from church as though we had kissed the Lord Jesus Christ, turning our face toward him. Will our people leave churches today like Isaiah left his worship experience in the temple, having a glimpse of the holiness of God, high and lifted up? Will we leave worship experiences as John did on Patmos when he had seen the glory of God and fell at his feet as a dead man?

These men were not entertained. They worshipped. Worship services today in so many ways are basically man-centered. In many churches you could pick up a bulletin from a worship service of 30 years ago and nothing would be different. We stand during the second hymn, because you want everyone standing for the prayer before the offering. That's just the way it's done. This is man-centered. We do something cute here. We entertain there, all seeking to please man. There is a virus in modern church that has a consuming desire to try to make everything friendly to people so they will not be offended.

What would happen if some people got desperate enough to make Christ the center of worship? More men and women might leave exclaiming what a wonderful savior. Fewer will leave exclaiming what a wonderful production, or what a funny, entertaining speaker.

Is God saying the same thing of our worship that he says in Isaiah 29:13 when God says, these people come near me with their mouths and they honor me with their lips, but their heart is far from me? Their worship of me is made up only of rules taught by men.

Hezekiah gives us an experience of shields of gold in worship. Look over at 2 Chronicles chapter 29. Remember, Ahaz has just gone "to sleep with his fathers." During Ahaz's rule, the Lord brought Judah low. Why? Because King Ahaz encouraged a moral decline in the land, and he was unfaithful, and he continued to be unfaithful to the Lord, continually. (2 Chronicles 28:19).

Now Hezekiah comes to the throne. In verse 2, we see that Hezekiah did what was right in the sight of the Lord.

He put up a new standard of excellence. In the first year of his reign, in the first month, he opened the doors of the house of the Lord and repaired them. He instigated change. He made worship a priority.

In verse 5, he said, "...sanctify yourselves, sanctify the house of the Lord your father, and carry out the rubbish from the holy place." He got rid of the rubbish. All the junk was removed from the place of worship.

Something interesting happens in verse 6. Hezekiah admits that their fathers had "done evil in the eyes of the Lord our God." That's a big thing to admit for a king, or for a super church. They turned their face away from the dwelling place of the Lord and turned their backs on Him. They also locked up the doors, turned out the lights and had not burned incense or offered offerings. Therefore, the wrath of the Lord fell upon Judah and Jerusalem, and he has given them up to trouble, to desolation and to jeering. This sounds familiar to me.

Has that happened to the church? Churches in a thousand cities no longer impact and engage their culture. Could it be that shields of brass have been substituted for shields of gold so long that God has repeated his judgment passed on the Southern Kingdom of Israel?

In 2 Chronicles 29:10-11, Hezekiah wants some relief. "Now it is in my heart to make a covenant with the Lord God of Israel that his fierce wrath may turn away from us. My son, do not be negligent now for the Lord has chosen you to stand before him. To serve him, that you should minister to him, and burn incense."

Here is commitment, getting with it. Do not put it off any longer. When we cease to substitute shields of gold, our promise is that we can look back and be able to say what is said in the last verse of chapter 29. "All the people rejoiced that God had prepared the people since the events took place so suddenly."

We call it prayer meeting. Is it? Or is it shields of brass for shields of gold? We call it Bible study–discipleship training–but is it? Really? Or is it shields of brass for shields of gold? How much real study and real training, is taking place?

The book of Acts records, that in the early church they continued steadfastly in teaching. Let us think again as if we were inventing the Christian church from scratch, with no knowledge of how to do it. The early Christians focused on teaching, corporate prayer time, and leadership training courses. This should be our model of reinstating the gold standard.

Much of what has been done the last few years in Bible study programs has just been a reaction to people or events. It has not been proaction. Reaction focuses on what happens to us in the past, proaction focuses on building for the future. I would like to see the church return to evangelism training, discipleship and Scripture memory. The goal is to develop healthy, strong believers, who in turn, can and will reproduce themselves in the lives of others.

We call it fellowship. Is it? Do we know much about New Testament koinonia? Body life? A large part of what every Sunday morning small-group Bible study should be is touching and ministering to the lives of one another.

We call it stewardship. Is it? I wonder what could happen if all the people of our churches were true stewards of God. Could we turn the tide? Would we have a standard of excellence in our stewardship?

We call those of us who are ministers, pastor. Are we? Every ministerial position on each church staff is an extension of the ministry of the pastor. In Peter's first epistle, he mentioned that ministers are to be three things.

We are to be an *episkopos*, a compound Greek word for one who gives oversight, one who leads, who has a vision for his particular area, who is proactive, who gives oversight to an area of ministry. Second, a *presbuteros*, one who has spiritual maturity in leading others. Third, he calls a minister a *poimein*, a shepherd, one who not only leads, but who feeds a group of people. You should be able to expect a pastor to give oversight, lead with spiritual maturity, and have a shepherd's heart as he leads and feeds the family of God. We ought to expect that of every minister on the staff.

Let's aim to assemble men and women on church staffs who have a high level of passion, whose passion index is turned up several notches: a group who can equip others to do the work of the ministry.

We call them deacons. Are we? The deacon, the *diakonos*, the foot-washer.

Scripture only describes two deacons in detail. One of them was Philip. He had a passion for God. He had a passion for the souls of men. It was Philip who drew near that chariot in the Gaza. There sat an Ethiopian eunuch who was wondering what he needed to do to know God. It was Philip who led him to faith in Christ. We also know it was Philip who went down to Caesarea and preached the Gospel of Jesus Christ, and who led his own family, every one of them, to be soul-winners. He had a passion.

Stephen is the other one. While in Jerusalem you can visit the Sheep's Gate—it's also called Stephen's Gate. It's called this because tradition says that Stephen was taken outside the city walls at this place when he was stoned to death. He died with a passion for people. He died leading people to Christ. He died praying for the souls of the people who were throwing rocks and cheering the mob.

I heard Johnny Oates, manager of the Texas Rangers, give his testimony. He would not have had that testimony except the providence of God that provided a deacon by the name of Bill Watts in Fort Lauderdale. One day during spring training Bill had the courage to approach Johnny Oates with the good news of Jesus Christ. He found Johnny Oates when God had been doing some things in his life, when Johnny was eager to hear anything that would bring hope. That day he embraced Jesus Christ as a personal savior.

We call it a church, but is it, or is it a shield of brass for a shield of gold? The church—the *ekklesia*—the called-out ones from the world. Are we perpetuating some dysfunctional programs that are no longer relevant for the sake of tradition instead of for purpose?

And the Gospel. Do we know what it is? Do we think it's good news? Do we really think it's the only way to heaven? Some of us must not really believe this or we would have more passion for our families and our lost friends. Each church member should want to be trained in evangelism, so that in the normal traffic patterns of life you can share a testimony—lead someone to Christ in your office. You can penetrate your culture. When you are at a soccer game and you meet a mom there in trouble, sitting right next to you. You can be equipped. We call them mission meetings. Are they? Sometimes we drive past a hundred mission opportunities to come to a church and talk about our love for great heroes of the faith like missionary physician Dr. Rebecca Naylor in Bangalore, India. In many places and in many ways, we have substituted shields of brass for shields of gold.

Chapter Four

The Standard of Excellence Restored

God's standard of excellence was restored in 2 Chronicles 12:12. When Rehoboam humbled himself, the wrath of the Lord turned from him so as not to completely destroy him. Things also went well with Judah. He humbled himself. That's a big thing for a king to do in front of his people. The correlating passage in 1 Kings 15:4-5: "Nevertheless, for David's sake, the Lord gave Rehoboam a lamp in Jerusalem."

God is more interested in excellence restored than we are. Verse 12 is a reminder of what we must do. To humble ourselves, admitting our need and our sin and doing something about it is a big pill for any church, especially a super church, to swallow.

The restoration challenge

What is your church going to look like in five years? Where are you going? How are you going to get there? We are responsible for a strategy for the future.

Many churches have not been proactive in years. We cannot hope that people will just come and sit in our services. Let us engage the culture. Let us write mission statements that give direction, aim and focus. Behind that, let us set some goals, some objectives and some initiatives.

No one wants to spend their life polishing brass to make it look like gold.

How do you make a comeback? Recently, I was reading a devotional on Jonah. Now there is a guy who came back. How did he do it? From the belly of a fish he says, "When my life was ebbing away, I remembered you, Lord. And my prayer rose to you in your holy temple" (Jonah 2:7). Those who cling to worthless idols forfeit the grace that could be theirs.

God has a standard of excellence for you personally, as a believer. Do not settle for anything less. Paul wrote about it in Philippians 3:8 "I count all things loss for the excellence of the knowledge of Christ Jesus my Lord." John put it like this in his first epistle: "Whoever keeps God's word truly the love of God is perfected and made excellent in him."

God's standard of excellence restored can take place in your life.

Part Two

Change is Not a Four Letter Word

Change is a necessity of life. Some churches are dead or dying today because they would not change. Change is a daily occurrence in our world and culture. Who would have thought, just a few years ago, that we would see the changes we have seen in the former Soviet Republic, or in Eastern Europe, or in the Middle East? Our own culture is changing as we enter the 21st century.

There are churches that are near death, with only a handful of people. These are not just small congregations of people. They are more like the people of another generation sitting quietly with a corpse in the parlor of a home waiting for the time of burial. These people are not engaging their culture, not impacting their world. They are just coming together in a little group that hunkers down within their four walls, and many of them are dead or dying because they are bound by tradition. Change is out of the question for many of them.

Russian cosmonaut Sergei Kreckolov was a member of the Communist Party. He was a confidante of Mikhail Gorbachev. He was privileged. In April of 1991 he was launched into space where he was to orbit the earth for four months in a Russian capsule.

While up there, his country's whole system of government collapsed. He was left up there. Nobody brought him back. He was finally brought back after ten months.

Imagine how he felt when he finally got home, only to find that home was nothing as it was when he was launched into space. Gorbachev had been deposed to his farm. Boris Yeltsin was now the leader of Russia. The Communist Party's dominance was history. His home town's name had been changed from Leningrad to St. Petersburg.

Sergei Kreckolov's true story is a parable of the human race. We are living in the greatest era of change in human history. We live in a world of computers, not industry. We live in a world of the Internet. Just a few short years ago the World Wide Web was only used by the CIA and the military. Now, anyone can have access to this worldwide system of information. One of the few things that Democrats and Republicans agree on is that every school student should have access to this information.

I recall when a church I pastored launched a home page on the web. We were so excited to be able to transmit our services live through the internet. Although someone lived halfway around the globe, our missionaries could go to church with us every Sunday if they had a computer with sound, a modem and internet service.

In the midst of a world of change we cannot live during the week with a 21st century mentality and expect to step back into a '50s world on Sunday morning and sing "We Shall Not Be Moved." Change is at the heart of everything Jesus had to say.

Take a look at Matthew 9:17. In this passage Jesus says, "Men do not take new wine and put it into old wineskins or else the wineskins will break, the wine is spilled, and the wineskins are ruined." When you put new wine into new wineskins, both are preserved. If there is one thing that can be said about our Lord Jesus Christ, it is that in the aftermath of his coming, he brought an incredible amount of change. This is what gave him so much trouble from the religious traditionalists of his day.

He shook things up. He broke with religious traditions as did his followers. At one point the Pharisees asked him point-blank, "Why do your disciples transgress the tradition of the elders?" (Matthew 15:2).

Do you know what was wrong with those religious Pharisees? They were not talking about the law. They were talking about the traditions of their elders. These religious traditions shackled the people with rules that had nothing to do with what their Bible said, and certainly not the message of the New Testment. The elders were upset about a tradition of washing their hands after every course of a meal. The disciples did not do it. The Bible never says to wash your hands after every course of a meal. But it bothered them that Jesus and his followers were not following, not the word of God, but the traditions that people had set down for them.

Do not misunderstand. Tradition is not a bad thing. It's a good thing in some ways. The Green Bay Packers like to play in the Super Bowl. Not just because it's the championship, but also because the Super Bowl trophy is named the Lombardi Trophy—

named after the former Green Bay coach Vince Lombardi. Don't you know they really want to bring home that trophy named after their former coach.

Most congregations have wonderful traditions. This is not necessarily a detriment. It can help us keep tethered to truth. Jesus is referring to man-made traditions that keep us shackled to the past. Jesus changed everything. After he came, worship changed. They even changed the day of worship. He was rejected for it. The religious traditionalists of his day did not like change.

Let's be honest. Change is difficult. Just about everybody is uncomfortable with change. Knowing this, I performed a little experiment at home. One Sunday our daughter, Wendy, was home from Baylor Law School. Holly was home from TCU with some of her friends. Susie prepared Sunday dinner for all of us after church. She had everything ready. Well, I was the first one into the room to sit down at the table. Purposefully, I sat on the side of the table opposite where I always sit.

We each sit at the same place every time we eat. Well, my wife, Susie came in and stopped. She looked at me and said, "What are you doing there?" At that moment Holly came in, and said, "Daaad!" I stayed there. You cannot imagine the commotion because I changed seats at the dinner table. People do not like change. Change is difficult.

Change feels different! Sometimes at the beginning we do not like it! That's what shook them up about Jesus Christ. He was not changing Scripture, he was coming to fulfill it. He was changing their stale institutionalism and the traditions they added to the

Scripture that caused them to be shackled and not relevant to a world in which they were living.

Jesus Christ is a change agent. Your church may be ready. Are you? When Jesus comes, he changes things. Look around you, he changes lives. He changes attitudes. He changes ideologies. Change is not a four letter word, and we do not have to be afraid of it.

Keep in mind two important components of our view of change. One of them is: Some things never change. The message never changes. The Good News of Jesus Christ never changes. Unapologetically, I will always hold to the complete trustworthiness, the authority, the infallibility, the inerrancy–whatever terminology you want to use–of the word of God. The Bible still says in Isaiah 40:8 that the *grass may wither, the flower may fade, but the word of God is what will stand forever.*

The second component of change: Some things always change. The way in which we translate that message, the relevancy in which we make known the Good News to a culture must always change. We need to always be changing our ministries, our methodologies, our styles in which we reach people. While the message never changes, the methods must!

Chapter Five

Option #1
Change Can Be Rejected

We can reject change. In the words of Jesus, in Matthew 9:17, men do not take new wine and put it into old wineskins because if they do, the new wine is still expanding, the gas is releasing and those old skins are brittle and cracking and cannot stretch. The skin will break and it'll be ruined. You cannot use it anymore for anything, and the wine will spill out and nobody will ever get the sparkling message of the Gospel.

So you can reject change, and cling to your old, brittle, cracked wineskins. That's what churches all over America have done. They are filled with a little handful of people. Why? They rejected change.

Contrary to popular opinion, strength is not in old methods. Strength is not in old wineskins. If they are not replaced with new wineskins we lose both the skin and the wine. Jesus speaks about wine in verse 17 as *oinos neos*, meaning recently made. The Greek words mean fresh, not fully fermented, still in the process of fermentation. It's still expanding. Its gases are still being released. Neos means new in reference to time, recent.

So we have this wine, brand new, still in the process of fermentation, still expanding. Next, Jesus talks about old wineskins. In the first century, wine was kept in goat skins. Goat skin is still an incredibly present thing in the Middle

East. You see it everywhere. Bedouin tents are made out of goat skins. It repels water and it holds water. The skin of the goat was removed without slitting it. Then, the openings of the feet from the skin were sewn up tightly and the neck portion of the skin was used for pouring. It formed a water-tight bag. To this day you can see these wineskins used by Bedouins all over the Middle East.

Jesus referred to the skins in this text as "old." He used the Greek word that means out-of-date, worn-out. Like an old shoe that has been bent out of shape and scuffed up with holes in the sole. That's the same Greek word they used to describe these skins. He said, do not take this wine that's still expanding and put it into these old wineskins. Old wineskins do not stretch. They lose elasticity, and become like an old piece of leather, brittle and cracked.

My first baseball glove was a genuine leather glove I got with S&H green stamps. I had a lot of other gloves. I played little league and had a new glove then. I got another glove the next year and then on up through junior high and high school. I probably had 10 or 12 baseball gloves by the time I got through my athletic career during my adolescence. Meanwhile, the old glove I got with those S&H green stamps had been forgotten and stuffed back in the garage at our old home place over on Crenshaw Street.

When Susie and I were about to be married, I went back over to clean out my things from my parents' house. I was going through the garage and reminiscing, looking through all these things, and I came across that first glove. I pulled it down off the shelf and tried to put my hand in it. I could not. It was so stiff and so brittle, my hand would not go in it. So I opened the pocket to look at it, and when I did, it cracked and pieces of it started peeling off.

That is what happens to old wineskins. That's what

Jesus is describing in verse 17. They get brittle and they begin to crack. You can imagine pouring new wine that's still expanding into one of these old skins.

If you reject change and try to use the same old wineskins that had elasticity in days gone by, but are now brittle and cracking, you are going to lose everything. You are going to lose the skin that still could be used for something. It's going to be ruined. And you are going to lose your message that you want to translate, whatever it is. This applies to anything, not just church business; anything. Both are going to be ruined.

If the Dallas Cowboys had used the same offensive schemes and defensive plays that they used in the early 1960s, they never would have won three Super Bowls in the 1990s. Their game—the message—was still the same. The methods and the strategies have changed. If Neiman Marcus carried the same merchandise today that they carried in the '60s, how long do you think they would stay in business? If you walked into Neiman Marcus today and they had not done one bit of remodeling since the 1960s how much business do you think it would do?

Billy Graham used the tent in his meetings. If he never changed and still used the tent as he did in 1949 in Los Angeles, what kind of success would he have had? In 1997 he used high-tech, modern satellite technology and preached to hundreds of millions of people in one service.

An article in our local paper told about recent successes of IBM. If IBM were still trying to market electric typewriters, how successful would they be? The purpose is the same, but the process is advanced.

We need new wineskins. In one church I pastored, the Sunday bulletin was a wineskin. I went into the library one week and looked at bulletins 30 years apart in age. They had the same type font, the same order of service, and virtually the same everything, just as it was in the 1960's. The bulletin is just a wineskin.

What I am saying is, like the Dallas Cowboys, Neiman Marcus and IBM, the Church of Jesus Christ needs to see the difference between its message which never changes— the wine—and its methods that should always be changing. If we reject change, listen to the results from the lips of Jesus himself. The wineskins break, the wine is spilled, and the wineskins are ruined.

The teaching of the grace of Jesus Christ does not have to be contained in the old forms and the old wineskins of the law. John 1:17 says, "For the law was given through Moses but grace and truth came through Jesus Christ." That was new wine! That's our new message! The Gospel, the Good News that Jesus came and suffered and died on a Roman cross for you. He did not just make a down payment for your sins. You do not have to come to him and work to try to pay the rest of it. He paid it in full to tell us it's finished. He was buried and rose again on the third day. That's the good news!

Two thousand years later, some people do not ever hear the good news because some of us are still trying to deliver it in wineskins that have lost their elasticity and are brittle and cracked.

Option number one, we can reject change, but if we do, we lose everything. You know, it's not hard to distinguish churches with old wineskins and those with new. In my experience, old wineskins are self-centered. The old wineskin churches want to be served. Those with new wineskins want to serve. Those with old wineskins exist for themselves. They are consumed with my church, my class and my room. Those with new wineskins exist for those who are not here yet, people who are in need outside the doors. Those with old wineskins enlist men and women they think can help them. Those with new wineskins go after people they think they can help.

Churches with old wineskins are no longer impacting the culture around them. They go on with programming and methodology that they used 30 years ago. Churches all over America are using the wineskins that their fathers and their grandfathers used and they are brittle and cracking and leaking today. The old-line institutional denominational churches, just name them one after another, are dying, and have little influence. You know why? Because they are too proud to change. Their wineskins that once worked wonderfully well when they had elasticity are breaking today and profusely leaking.

The fallacy is they still think their strength is in old wineskins. Well, it worked back in 1960, why can't we just do what we did back then? The only hope for these churches, my church and your church, is to incorporate new wineskins to hold the sparkling message of the Gospel that must be shared with a thirsty world. Jesus is simply saying, without change, you are going to lose the message and the methods. One would never put new wine into old wineskins.

So what is the wine? It's the new covenant. It's the Gospel. It's the Good News. It's what the thirsty world needs. What is the wineskin? It's what we hold it in. It's the methodology, the way in which we take the message to the world.

Old wineskins are often found in antiquated philosophies, in stale institutionalism, and bureaucratic denominationalism. We are prone to think that our strength is in old wineskins because they once served us well. There are some men and women who are bound by thought patterns of the past. They are conditioned against change. Many leaders are chained to the stake of traditionalism and resist change. Thus when pressure to change emerges, their old wineskins, now brittle and cracking, eventually burst. They spill the message that the world so desperately needs to hear. We also may lose those skins. The very existence of the church is threatened.

The wine is the message. The skin is the method. The wine is the truth, which never changes. The skin is the tradition. The wine is the revelation. The skin is the relevancy. The wine is the content of the Gospel. The skin is the container. What is important is the message, but the world—the thirsty world—is never going to get the message if we are losing it in old wineskins.

A new generation of children is being raised in a high-tech, visual world. Before they even start to school they know how to use computers, three-dimensional computer graphics. Now, we bring them to Sunday schools to listen to a one-dimensional lesson and we wonder why they cannot connect. I look forward to the day when every children's department is equipped with some high-tech visual aids in order to present Bible truth that connects with these young minds, and when possible, worship in an auditorium designed for the 21st century.

We can respect change. Jesus says when we do, both the message and the skins are preserved.

Consider an elephant with that chain on his ankle. He is staked down there. Although the animal is strong enough to pull it out of the ground, he will not move because he is conditioned against moving. He will not walk away. Why? Because of a pre-conditioned mind set against change. Just like a powerful elephant, a lot of churches are constrained by old wineskins of pre-conceived and archaic methodology.

However, there is something that will cause an elephant to pick up that chain and blast off with power and run away. When he smells smoke or sees a fire. When that happens, all pre-conditioned mind sets are forgotten. Let the circus tent catch fire, and the elephant smells a little smoke. He will pull up that stake and he will be gone.

In your church you may not see any fire yet. Can you smell the smoke? There are a lot of people that are praying. Many of our young people are leaving our churches because we cannot connect with them. There are a lot of people who are ready. There are a lot of people who are waiting for new wineskins.

We are going to see the fire. Can you smell the smoke? God is moving. It's time for us to pull up some of our old stakes and get going. Can you smell it? Jesus said, "Listen, don't put new wine into old skins. If you do, when those gases start expanding and those skins can't stretch, when they've lost their elasticity and they're brittle, they will crack and break open. Then, the skin will not be good for anything. Then, the wine will be spilled out and the world will never hear my message." He said to change. Put new wine into some new skins, and when you do, both will be preserved. Change is not a four-letter word.

Chapter Six

Option #2 Change Can Be Respected

If anybody's ever read the reports of the revival that swept the Hebrides Islands, you know that the agent of that revival was a man named Duncan Campbell. One day while in his study, his daughter came in and said, "Daddy, things aren't like they used to be between you and God, are they?" Duncan Campbell began to pray that God would bring back the glory.

Change. It's not a four letter word. Jesus said in Matthew 9:17 that men do not take new wine and put it into old wineskins. Take new wine, Jesus says, and put it into new wineskins. Look at the result. Both are preserved.

Jesus says change is a necessity. He says there comes a time in the life of an individual or an entity when you have to take the new wine—the unchanging message of the Gospel—and put it into new wineskins. Change is difficult whether it is around our house or around our church or around our office or anywhere around our being.

Somebody said to me, Pastor, there is only one group of people in this church that like change. It's those babies in the nursery. They like to be changed.

The mother eagle hatches her young and she raises those little eaglets in the nest. They grow in the nest located high up on some rocky cliff or in the top of a tall tree. The mother eagle protects them, provides for them, feeds them, until there comes a day of change. Dramatic change. I am sure her heart pounds within her breast with conflicting emotions as she takes her beak and nudges each of her offspring to the edge of the nest.

Why does the thrill of soaring always have to begin with the fear of falling? That's an age-old question. So there they are in the security of their nest located high on the face of some sheer rock cliff. Below there is nothing but air to support wings that have never been tried. The mother's parental mission is now complete, except for one final task. The push.

Even eagles need a push. Incidentally, that is also the popular title of an outstanding business book by David McNally—"Yes, Even Eagles Need a Push!" Unless those young eaglets discover their wings, there is no purpose for their lives. Unless they learn to soar, they will fail to learn the privilege of being an eagle. Many churches are nestled comfortably in their nests—never doing what God has designed and commanded them to do. Never fulfilling their purpose. The push! Out of the nest! It is the greatest gift the mother can give her young eagles. The greatest gift.

The push to maturity is the supreme act of love and survival. So, one by one, the eagle pushes her young out of the nest until it falls. But then, it flies. And another—she pushes and he falls, but then he flies, and they all begin to mount up, as Isaiah said, with wings as eagles as they were designed to do, and they soar.

We have been nesting in our churches some time. I am convinced that our Lord is nudging us now to the edge of the nest. He himself is giving us a push. It is the supreme act of love and survival. Oh, the fear of falling is real, but to soar is to mount up, as the prophet says, with wings like eagles, and to be what God has intended us to be, to engage, and impact, and convert this culture. The thrill of soaring. Even eagles need a push. Change is not a four letter word. We are faced with two options. *Stay in the nest of a comfort zone and die, or soar once again for God's glory.* I am not too sure we even really have an option. I think God is pushing us out. Jesus said, "Listen, men do not take the new wine of this message of the Gospel and put it into old wineskins. They will break and the message will be lost and the methods will be lost. No, we take new wine and we put it into new wineskins and then both are preserved."

We can try to keep holding the message of the Gospel in a bunch of old wineskins that are leaking profusely and breaking, and we are losing the message. It's not getting out to the world. We are losing the skins in the process. Many churches in America are headed for empty. They have but a handful of people in their nest today. They're using old wineskins that their fathers and their grandfathers used in other generations, but today they're brittle and they're cracking and they're leaking. These wineskins worked so wonderfully well in the '50s and '60s, and some of them still think that their strength is in old wineskins. So they hold on to them and in the process they lose the message that needs to get out to a lost and dying world. Jesus is simply saying, without change you are going to lose it all.

What is the wine? It's the message. It never changes. It's the Gospel. What is the Gospel? That Jesus suffered on a Roman cross outside the city walls of Jerusalem. He who knew no sin bore your sin in his own body on the cross. He died on the Roman cross. He was buried and three days later he arose from the grave, the living, triumphant Lord and Savior. That's the message the world needs and it never changes. That's the wine.

Jesus said take new wine that's still in the fermentation

process and put it in the new skins, and both are preserved. Jude 3, says this unchanging message is *the faith once for all delivered to the saints.*

In Matthew 9:17, Jesus mentions new wine. It's new in the sense that it's recently been made, and not fully fermented. It's still in the process of fermentation. Now, he mentions new wineskins as opposed to the old ones. When he speaks of new wine and new wineskins, he uses a different Greek word to describe the new wineskins from that which he uses when he talks about the new wine.

When he speaks of new wineskins he does not use *neos*, he uses a Greek word *kainos* which means that it's not so much *new in time*, as it is *new in quality*. New as opposed to that which has already seen service.

The best way I think you could translate it is, fresh. New in character. Look at these new wineskins. They are truly different. They are fresh, they are flexible. They have elasticity. They have not been used before.

Jesus is saying that change is necessary to get his message out, the new wine needs new wineskins. The new wine expanding in the fermentation process stretches those skins, and consequently, new wine needs to be contained from time to time, from generation to generation, in new wineskins with elasticity. The old ones have already been stretched to the limit. They're cracking, they're brittle, and the fermentation process causes leaks and you lose the message. The world does not hear the message. That's why the world's not hearing the message from most churches in America. It's not because they do not have the message, it's because they do not have it contained in new wineskins that can pour out to a world that will listen. They have lost both, the message and the methods.

Do you remember the Oldsmobile advertising slogan–

This is not my father's Oldsmobile? They were saying, to a younger generation, you think Oldsmobiles are for fuddy-duddies because your old dad drove that Oldsmobile with a stodgy image. It was an old person's car. Think again. This isn't your dad's Oldsmobile. This one is new. It's not what you remember. This one has cruise control and CD stereo and all sorts of airbags and all kinds of sleek lines.

The problem today is that a new generation feels the church is their father's Oldsmobile. You know why? Because almost everything in most churches is geared to their father's generation.

If anyone ought to pick up that Oldsmobile jingle, it ought to be the Church of Jesus Christ. There are a couple of generations of the church today that are out there away from the church because many of our methods have not changed since my dad bought a General Motors car in 1963. Methods, like wineskins, that once worked are now old and brittle. The church of the new millennium ought to be in some ways as different as the church in the '60s, as the automobile that you purchase today is as different from the automobile that you purchased 30 years ago.

The purpose of automobiles has not changed in all those years. The purpose is still to transport you. It's still to get you from point A to point B. The wine has not changed, but the skins have, for a new generation. The purpose of the church has not changed. The message never changes. The purpose of the church is to give glory and honor to Jesus Christ and to fulfill the Great Commission. However, the wineskins ought to change, and tragically, in many churches they have not. They have not translated it to a new generation. The Church of Jesus Christ is in desperate need of new wineskins today.

We do not need modern theology. We have the faith

once for all delivered to the saints. We do need to contain it in modern methodology. The wine is the same in the first part of verse 17 and the second part of verse 17. The wineskins are what changed.

When we read the Book of Acts we see the early church exploding in growth. They engaged a pagan, godless culture like ours. They exploded in Ephesus and Corinth and everywhere they went. Paul was wise enough to know the skins that worked in the Jerusalem church in a Jewish culture would not work in Corinth and in other pagan Greek cultures. He took that new wine and he put it into new wineskins. In fact, all through the church age this is what happened. When we find the church discovering new life, when we find the church engaging and impacting its culture, you will find the church changing. Putting on some new wineskins. Not changing their message, but the methods that hold the truth.

In the 16th century the new wine of the Reformation could not be held in the old wineskins of stale institutionalism and of the papacy. They poured new wine into new wineskins and they were called heretics for doing it, and some of them lost their lives. We call them Reformers. Churches all over—especially the Western world—meet to worship Christ today because of them.

What is our Lord saying to us? He is saying without change both the message and the methods are going to be lost. With change both are going to be preserved. The bottom line is, change is a necessity; it's not an option to engage each generation and each new culture. We need to stop wasting time trying to patch up old wineskins. This is a day of new opportunity. If we become relevant we are going to have to respect change. Like eagles we need a push.

We must dare to chart new paths, and pioneer new ministries that had never been performed before. Some young couples left our churches in recent years because they felt it was their father's Oldsmobile. Should we be surprised that contemporary music is rejected today by a large segment of traditional culture and traditional churches? It always has been so; always. After awhile, the new music becomes traditional. What we call traditional is what someone else a few years ago called contemporary. All music is contemporary at one time or another. It's difficult to write an old song.

In 1965 when I was a teenager our church youth group in Fort Worth was going to camp. We were going to make a contemporary song, "All to Thee," our theme song. Some of the people did not want to use that as the camp theme because it was not in the hymnal. If you look in your hymnal today, you will find the hymn, "All to Thee." It's now a traditional hymn.

Martin Luther took the secular melodies of his day, which everyone enjoyed singing together—they called it a chorale—and he emphasized popular, secular tunes for worship. Luther asked *Why should the devil have all the good tunes?* One of our traditional hymns "A Mighty Fortress Is Our God" was a secular tune of his day.

Or take the Wesleys, John and Charles. Here are some traditional hymns that we love. "Oh, for a Thousand Tongues to Sing Our Great Redeemer's Praise." "And Can It Be." Hymns like "Love Divine, All Loves Excelling, Joy of Heaven to Earth Come Down." These songs were scoffed at by the traditionalists in Wesley's day. They said they came from the tunes of the beer gardens in Europe, and they did. Wesley took tunes that he heard men and women singing in the fields and singing in jails. He took those tunes and equipped them with a Christian message. Today we call it traditional. The secular became the sacred.

Isaac Watts is the father of English hymnody. "Joy to the World, The Lord Has Come." "When I Survey the Wondrous Cross on Which the Prince of Glory Died." He led the church out of the bondage of singing strict psalmody. It was radical stuff. Isaac Watts took tunes and melodies from folk music of his day and brought them into the church. A lot of people did not like that contemporary stuff that we call traditional today.

In America, old Appalachian folk tunes found their way into the church. You don't remember Samuel Stinnett, but you certainly have sung a song he wrote—"On Jordan's stormy banks I stand and cast a wishful eye to Canaan's fair and happy land where my possessions lie." Radical stuff. That was an Appalachian mountain folk tune and the church was repulsed by it.

Some contemporary expressions today should not be rejected. There is a new wind of excellence blowing in a contemporary approach. We have a culture to reach for Christ. Our missionaries taught us years ago that if we reach people, we have to cross cultural barriers to do it. We cannot try to take our own culture and impose it on them and win them to Christ. We do not do that on the mission field, and unless you have not realized it yet, we are in a mission field, a pagan culture, in the United States.

If we were in an African culture today, we would have bongo drums. If we were over in Scotland, we would have bagpipes. We are in a 21st century American culture that knows nothing of Jesus Christ. We have the message but we are not going to reach today's culture with the same approach that our fathers and our grandfathers used. Contemporary is here and change is not a four-letter word.

I prefer hymns. I am always going to prefer hymns because of their theological import, their devotional nature. I memorize them. I cannot imagine my personal devotion time without repeating hymns of praise to God. We call them traditional, but once they were all new. God gives each generation musical expressions of praise. God did not quit giving the world new songs when Fanny Crosby died. He is still doing it today. We talk about the old hymns of our faith like "Have faith in God when your pathway is lonely." B.B. McKinney from Fort Worth wrote that in 1934. The church lasted 19 centuries without what we call the old hymns of our faith. Most of them are written in the last hundred years.

Hymns are cultural wineskins themselves. What does "Let the Lower Lights Be Burning" have to say to a 21st century generation? What young adult knows today what that song means? It was written before air travel, it was written before electricity. When fog set in around a harbor, the ships needed a way to direct them to the dock. Along the bottom of the harbor, they would light lanterns below the fog to direct the ship's captain. Let the lower lights be burning, send a gleam across the way, some poor struggling, fainting seaman you may rescue, you may save. What does that song say to a 21st century world that knows nothing about sea travel?

Today's culture knows something about lower lights today, but they are on runways of airports. These are wineskins. This is a different culture. When I speak of musical wineskins I do not mean that we should abandon hymns. We need new, fresh hymns of expression that speak the language of a new generation. That's what we did in the past when we were on the cutting edge. It's what we must do in the future as we leave this culture warp, as we are nudged out of this nest. Is it unthinkable that God could inspire hymns that identify with hot air balloons, roller blades and compact disks?

In our churches, we are different in age, we are different in socio-economic levels, we have different tastes, we have different aesthetic values, we have different educational levels. We are different in a thousand ways. Music is not what unites us. The Lord Jesus Christ is what ought to unite us. We are living in a market-driven niche society that leads us to believe that we must have things our way. Old wineskins.

Susie and I were visiting a young couple that had been to our church. As we sat in their den talking, their 3-year-old daughter came into the room, pulled out a CD, placed it in the CD ROM drive, sat down at the computer and began to play a video game. As she played, the software reacted to what she was doing by talking to her. For 30 minutes she played this beautiful, multi-colored, three-dimensional video game.

That's what children are doing today. When they come to Sunday School, they sit down for an hour in a class with somebody trying to teach a Bible lesson with a one-dimensional flannel board. We wonder why they are lost and bored. Wineskins.

We need to have every children's department equipped with computer equipment. There are all sorts of new biblical games being created. Children can learn Bible stories on the computer, in the same way they are learning other lessons in their homes. New wineskins, reaching a new world for Christ.

How are we going to reach this world? Seven-eighths of the world in the 1960s had some kind of church background. Today, one-eighth have some kind of church background.

It's a different world. In the "olden days" of the 60s, families were like the television shows of the day. Ozzie and Harriet. Leave it to Beaver. Not so today. When I think about the family today, half of the people to whom we are speaking are single parents. Many others are blended families. It's a different world. In our changing culture, many churches are still trying to reach this world with a *Leave it to Beaver mentality.* Ward does not come home at 5 o'clock every afternoon anymore, if he comes home at all. June is not scurrying around the house all day with a little white apron, having cookies and milk ready for the Beaver when he gets in from school. Teenage Wally's biggest problem is not the sarcasm of his friend Eddie Haskell. And the Beaver? He is not getting into trouble for chewing gum at school.

Ward Cleaver of the 21st century seldom sits down to eat a meal with his family. June is a single mom in more cases than not. Wally is facing all sorts of temptations as a young teenager; he is being handed condoms in his school by adults. There are all kinds of temptations that teenagers in the '60s never even dreamed about. Beaver comes home from elementary school to an empty house and sits in front of a computer and gets on the Internet and sees some of the most vulgar images you have ever seen in your life. That is the real world.

Our challenge is to put our arms around this world and bring these people to our Savior. He has commanded us to do that, and we do not need to react to them. We need to engage them by packaging the Gospel in some new wineskins.

What does this say to us? We must show respect for some needed changes in style and substance. Our old message is still new. It's the Good News. We must see some new wineskins in style and ministry. Our Sunday Schools must become what they once were—entry ports for evangelism. Our youth and singles' ministries cannot sit around waiting for people to come to us; we need strategies to engage these campuses, to get out there and engage our culture with new wineskins.

Think of the implications that can be made at this point. Some of you have what you call supper clubs. I think they are wonderful. It's koinonia, fellowship in the truest biblical sense. You share your life and the life of Christ with many lifelong friends. We need fellowship with one another. This world needs and wants relationships.

What would happen in our churches if we added to that type of supper club one like Matthew had in Capernuum in Luke 5 when he was saved? Matthew gave Christ a great feast in his own house and he invited a great number of tax collectors and others who sat down with him. In fact, it was at that dinner that the context of this chapter on wineskins emerged. Matthew gathered his friends and his business associates for the expressed purpose of introducing them to Jesus Christ. What would happen if couples from your church opened their home to their neighbors and business associates for a dinner? Perhaps you could show a ten-minute video that the church prepared or some other method.

How can we move from rhetoric to reality? Each of us has to start looking for ways to share the gospel. Our old men dreaming new dreams, our young men seeing new visions, as the prophet said; all of us pouring new wine into new wineskins.

The push, the risk, the fall of the young eagle, and then something hit him in the face. The winds of change blowing

against him. What will he do with this? Does he let these
winds of change plummet him to the ground and crash?
No! He uses them to his advantage. The strong winds create
a thermal updraft and cause him to just set his wings and
soar higher than he ever thought he could soar with so little
effort. His wings are designed to glide into those strong
winds of change. Not only can he soar even higher than
that nest, but faster, and longer than he ever dreamed.

The eagle would never have known he could soar
without the push. The push! Jesus is saying to his church,
you have been nesting long enough. I designed you to soar.
Jesus Christ is nudging. He is pushing us. It's the supreme
act of love and survival. He is pushing for our good, but
ultimately for his glory. Even eagles need a push.

Susie and I went into the Garden of Gethsemane to a
private place that a caretaker once showed us. Tourists are
not allowed in this specific area but it is believed to be the
place that Jesus prayed the night he was arrested. We have
been to this place several times to pray. This time we were
coming to pray over the decision to leave Fort Lauderdale
and go to the First Baptist Church of Dallas. There is a
particular rock where for years we have met God in prayer.
We sat there, prayed and read the passion narratives. When
we came to the passage of the Gethsemane experience, I
was struck by the words, *Lord, if it's possible, let this cup
pass from me*, like never before.

I did not want to leave my church. Nevertheless, not
my will but Thine be done. We made a commitment to
Christ in that garden. We sensed God's spirit saying go,
and we never looked back. Recently, I went back to that
rock, to pray again. It was early morning. I noticed that
dew was everywhere. I picked a blade of grass covered
with dew. Then, I remembered a scripture that I memorized

long ago.

In Hosea 14:5 *God said, "I will be like the dew to Israel."* Where does dew come from? Does dew fall? Or does dew rise? Neither. Water vapor condenses on a cool place, usually at night when conditions are right. You see, dew does not fall, and dew does not rise. It just appears when conditions are right. *God said I will be like the dew to my people. He will just appear when conditions are right!*

When we see God's standard of excellence revealed. When we admit God's standard of excellence has been removed. When we acknowledge God's standard of excellence has been replaced. When we come to the place where God's standard of excellence is restored. *When conditions are right, God just appears, and the blessing of God comes. God said, I will be as the dew to my people. When conditions are right, I will show up.*

The power of God comes in such a fashion that folks stand by and say, that was not marketing, that was not public relations—*that can only be the power of God.* Change is not a four letter word!

Part Three

Four Pillars of Biblical Church Growth

What makes a church great? This question is dependent upon whether we are referring to a great church in the eyes of people or a great church in the eyes of God. Often in the eyes of people a great church is determined by a stupendous financial program. However, there are many churches with huge endowments which are dead and listless.

Others might claim that vast physical facilities make a great church. While this may be true from people's views, there are churches with mammoth, magnificent edifices with only a handful of people. You can find in the downtown areas of most major cities, churches that were once vibrant and alive that are now dead or dying, but with awe-inspiring physical facilities. Still others would insist that a great church is made up of those with elite social standing. While such a church may be called great by people, it is not necessarily so in the eyes of God.

The secret to a great church in the eyes of God is found in the second chapter of Acts with the birth of the church. It includes four vital elements. The first element is *participation.* These early believers were "all together" (Acts 2:1) and they were "all filled" (Acts 2:4). They found their strength in participation with each other (unity) and in participation with God (unction). There has never been a great church that has not captured this element of participation.

Second, there is the element of *proclamation.* In a day when young preachers are encouraged to preach short topical messages, it should be remembered that these early believers preached the Word of God. Peter stood up on the day of Pentecost, took a text from the scroll of Joel, and preached the gospel of Jesus Christ, boldly and unashamedly.

Third, there is the element of *preservation.* The Bible tells us they "continued steadfastly" in the apostles' teachings. They "devoted themselves" to prayer and fellowship. People did not come through one door of the early church and out the back. There was none of this anonymity that is the calling card of many modern churches. There was none of this idea of avoiding doctrinal truth in order to make the message more palatable to a wide variety of wants. They had captured the element of preservation.

Finally, there is the element of *propagation.* We live and minister in a day when many churches even advertise the promise that they will not visit you. The early believers went everywhere witnessing, and the Bible states, "the Lord added to their number daily those who were being saved" (Acts 2:47). Any church that aspires to be great in the eyes of God must be characterized by these four vital elements.

Today, the church of the Lord Jesus Christ must raise up her head and remember who she is. I hope we do not want to be viewed in our cities as some kind of religious, country club or some sort of second-class organization that is thrown a bone from the city's civic community from time to time. No! The church is not some insignificant, musty-smelling mausoleum trying to hold onto a few traditional values of the past. The most important organization to the future of any area ought to be the local New Testament church. It ought not to be the Tourist Bureau, the Chamber of Commerce, the Downtown Development Authority, or any other such organizations. It ought to be the local New Testament church planted in the heart of the community, making a difference for Jesus' sake.

The church was born in the city of Jerusalem in the first-century AD. People from all over the known world gathered there for the Feast of Pentecost. As many as one million Jews descended upon the city for the annual celebration. But on that particular day, 120 believers became the center of attention. The Feast of Pentecost had been observed for 1,500 years. Always held fifty days after the Passover, it was designed to celebrate the arrival of the Israelites to Mount Sinai after their deliverance from Egypt. During that feast God had the attention of the city and ultimately the world, and through one local body of believers, turned the world upside down. How the church ought to pray in these days, "Lord, do it again!"

I repeat, "What makes a church great in the eyes of God?" Participation, proclamation, preservation, and propagation make it great. Every church ought to exhibit all four. There are some churches which have participation but no proclamation. Others are strong on proclamation but have no participation. Others have participation and proclamation but no preservation. Others have the first three but no program of propagation of the gospel. Great churches are known by balanced ministries and have all four elements found in Acts 2. They live together in love and unity, are filled with the Holy Spirit, make much of the Word of God, have ministries to preserve new converts, and continue to exist for those beyond their four walls.

Chapter Seven

Participation

The members of the early church found their strength in participation with one another. They were "all together" (Acts 2:1). They were united and not divided. They decided to stay together as well as pray together. Unity is one of the single most important factors in church growth. We are talking about unity and not uniformity. Cults emphasize uniformity, while the church emphasizes unity. The church is the picture of a quartet with each member singing different parts of the same song but blending together in perfect harmony.

What was the real phenomenon occurring on the day the church was born? It was a miracle of sound and sight. There was a miracle of *sound:* "Suddenly a sound like the blowing of a violent wind came from heaven and filled the whole house where they were sitting" (Acts 2:2). The *sound* of the wind was the sign of the Holy Spirit. Earlier Jesus taught in his conversation with Nicodemus, "The wind blows wherever it pleases. You hear its sound, but you cannot tell where it comes from or where it is going. So it is with everyone born of the Spirit" (John 3:8). There was also the miracle of *sight.* "They saw what seemed to be tongues of fire that separated and came to rest on each of them" (Acts 2:3). There were cloven tongues of fire which, like the wind, was the sign of the Holy Spirit. Fire that consumes. Oh, how our Lord desires to consume us as His church.

There is plenty of talk in church circles today about

seeing Pentecost repeated. How many times have we heard phrases such as, "They had a Pentecost at such and such church." If Pentecost is repeated there will be some signs. We will hear the sound of a rushing, mighty wind and see cloven tongues of fire appearing above each head. People will speak in *glossa* (languages) and *dialektos* (dialects). Why are we not seeing this phenomenon in the church today? There is no need for Pentecost to be repeated. It was a one-time event.

The coming of the Holy Spirit to indwell the believers and never to leave them, just like Bethlehem, was a one-time event and never needs to be repeated. It was like Calvary which was a one-time event and never needs to be repeated. Pentecost is the same. At Bethlehem, we see God *with* us. At Calvary, we see God *for* us. At Pentecost, we see God *in* us. For a Christian to pray, "Lord, send the Holy Spirit just like you did on the Day of Pentecost," would be the same as praying, "Lord, send Jesus to Bethlehem to be born of a virgin." He already has. It would be the same as praying, "Lord, send Jesus out to Calvary to die on a cross for our sins." He already has! Pentecost was a onetime event when the Holy Spirit came to indwell the believers, never to leave them and to empower them for service.

Note that the blessing on the Day of Pentecost came "suddenly" (Acts 2:2). It was not obtained through a process of growth or development. No one taught anyone else how to do what happened. It did not evolve out of one's own mental attitudes. It was the sovereign, supernatural gift of the Father upon each person. No one was excluded (see Acts 2:3). It was not manifested by merit. It was the work of God. It came "suddenly;" and the effect was that "all of them were filled with the Holy Spirit" (Acts 2:4).

One of the problems of today's church is that it has lost

its expectancy. It is amazing how many events came about in the early church "suddenly." They seemed to live in anticipation of the unexpected. In Acts 2 the early believers were not waiting until they became worthy. They were praying and waiting, and "suddenly" the Spirit came.

Think of the shepherds living in the fields, keeping watch over their flocks at night:

An angel of the Lord appeared to them, and the glory of the Lord shone around them, and they were terrified. The angel said to them, "Do not be afraid. I bring you good news of great joy that will be for all the people. Today in the town of David a Savior has been born to you; he is Christ the Lord. This will be a sign to you: You will find a baby wrapped in strips of cloth and lying in a manger."

Suddenly a great company of the heavenly host appeared with the angel, praising God and saying, "Glory to God in the highest, and on earth peace to men on whom his favor rests" (Luke 2:9-14, author's italics).

Think of the apostle Paul on the Damascus road. The Bible records:

Meanwhile, Saul was still breathing out murderous threats against the Lord's disciples. He went to the high priest and asked him for letters to the synagogues in Damascus, so that if he found any there who belonged to the Way, whether men or women, he might take them as prisoners to Jerusalem. As he neared Damascus on his journey, *suddenly* a light from heaven flashed around him (Acts 9:1-3, author's italics).

Think of Silas and Paul in prison at Philippi. The Bible records:

About midnight Paul and Silas were praying and singing hymns to God, and the other prisoners were listening to them. *Suddenly* there was such a violent earthquake that the foundations of the prison were shaken. At once all the prison doors flew open, and everybody's chains came loose (Acts 16:25-26, author's italics).

Oh, the possibility of those of us who live in the realm of expecting the unexpected!

On the day the church was born, the believers were "all together in one place" (Acts 2:1). They sensed a ministry of attendance. They had felt that ministry since earlier in the upper room when Thomas was "not there when Jesus came." Now, they were in their place, "all together in one place." The church today would sense more power if its members lived in anticipation and were all together in one place.

Every layperson in every church has a ministry of attendance. One of the saddest verses in all the Bible is recorded in John 20:24 where the Scripture reveals, "Thomas...was not with the disciples when Jesus came." How urgent it is to be in one's place at the time of worship. I have often wondered where Thomas was that day. Wherever he was, was not really the central concern; the point is, he was *not where he should have been when Jesus came.* Like Thomas, we are missing out when we are not fulfilling our ministry of attendance. The Lord brought not only His *presence* into the group that day, but also His *peace.* One never knows when he is not in his place if Jesus will pass by in tremendous power and presence. I am convinced that the actual reason Thomas was not there when Jesus came was the identical reason so many people in so many churches today do not fulfill their ministry of attendance. They simply do not expect Jesus to be there! A large percentage of church members attend as if they were going to some sort of concert or town council meeting, without any thought that Jesus is actually passing by. Each of us has an awesome responsibility and a "ministry of attendance" at our own local church.

One of the real characteristics of the first-century church was unity. They were in one accord, in one place. In fact, it is amazing how, as we read through the Book of Acts, they continued to find their strength in participation with each other. They began in Acts 1:14: "They all joined together constantly in prayer, along with the women and Mary the mother of Jesus, and his brothers." They continued in Acts 2:1: "When the day of Pentecost came, they were all together in one place." After the day of Pentecost the Bible records, "Every day they continued to meet together in the temple courts. They broke bread in their homes and ate together with glad and sincere hearts" (Acts 2:46).

After Peter and John had been arrested, the Bible emphasizes, "When they heard this, they raised their voices together in prayer to God. 'Sovereign Lord; they said, 'you made the heaven and the earth and the sea, and everything in them'"(Acts 4:24). When deep fear came upon them after the death of Ananias and Sapphira the Bible records, "The apostles performed many miraculous signs and wonders among the people. And all the believers used to meet together in Solomon's Colonnade" (Acts 5:12). The secret to the growth of the early church was its living together in love and unity.

The most important fact is not what they saw or heard

but that they were "all together." They were in one accord, and God met them in that place. Participation, unity, and unction were manifest. They were as different as people in churches today, but God cemented them together and did great and mighty works through them. Look at those in that group. Peter was there. He was so boisterous and the one who denied our Lord before a maiden. Thomas the doubter was present. John and James were in the midst, having been so selfish in wanting to have the number one and number two positions in the Kingdom. There were forgiven adulterers and also tax collectors. You name it, and they were there-Joseph of Arimathea and civic leaders like Nicodemus. They were all different but their secret was they were "all together" in one place. There was participation in unity. They found strength in participation with each other.

Unity was the key to the outpouring of God's Spirit. This group was so diverse. Probably much more diverse than most churches are today. They had the richest of the rich in Joseph of Arimathea and the poorest of the poor in the widow. Yet, they were "all together." There seemed to be no petty bickering, no silly jealousy, no bragging of certain socio-economic groups to the exclusion of others. So many churches today are filled with people who are backbiting and murmuring. Many of us ought to stop worrying about getting a blessing and start worrying about being a blessing. The secret of this Jerusalem church was participation. They found their strength in participation with one another. This is the real key to a great church in the eyes of God. Unity was the theme. They were "all together in one place."

They not only found their strength in participation with one another, but in participation with God. *"All* of them were filled with the Holy Spirit" (Acts 2:4, author's italics). Not some of them but all of them! They had been baptized, indwelt, and sealed by the Holy Spirit; now they were filled by Him. The emphasis in Acts 2 is on the filling of the Holy Spirit. This puts us under the spotlight of the principle of "being before doing;' for what we do is always determined by who we are and what we are. While baptism with the Holy Spirit was a once-and-for-all encounter, the filling of the Holy Spirit is to be repeated over and over again. This is what makes a church great in the eyes of God—a Spirit-filled membership where Jesus is the Lord of every life. At conversion we have the Holy Spirit. When we are filled, the Holy Spirit has us!

The work of the Holy Spirit in our lives involves several factors. It involves the *baptism with the Holy Spirit.* First Corinthians 12:13 says: "For we were all baptized by one Spirit into one body—whether Jews or Greeks, slave or free—and we are all given the one Spirit to drink."

There is also the *indwelling of the Holy Spirit.* Romans 8:9 says: "You, however, are controlled not by the sinful nature but by the Spirit, if the Spirit of God lives in you. And if anyone does not have the Spirit of Christ, he does not belong to Christ."

Then there is the *sealing of the Holy Spirit.* Ephesians 1:13-14 states: And you also were inducted in Christ when you heard the word of truth, the gospel of your salvation. Having believed, you were marked in him with a seal, the promised Holy Spirit, who is a deposit guaranteeing our inheritance until the redemption of those who are God's possession—to the praise of his glory.

Next comes the *filling of the Holy Spirit* found in Ephesians 5:18: "Do not get drunk on wine, which leads to debauchery. Instead, be filled with the Spirit." The filling is conditional upon our surrender to Jesus as Lord.

There is also the *anointing of the Holy Spirit.* At the Lord's baptism, the Holy Spirit anointed Him. The anointing is a special touch for a special task. Thank God for the anointing! No preacher ought to preach without asking God for "fresh oil"—the anointing. No singer ought to sing without asking God for the anointing. No teacher ought to teach the Bible without asking God for the anointing.

What is the command of the Bible concerning the Holy Spirit? Is it to be *baptized* with the Holy Spirit? No! There is not one command in Scripture to be baptized with the Holy Spirit. If we are saved, the Bible teaches us we have already been baptized with the Holy Spirit. Are we commanded to be *indwelt* by the Holy Spirit? No! Is the command, then, to be *sealed* with the Holy Spirit? Again, the answer is no. The command of Scripture concerning the Holy Spirit is to "be filled with the Spirit" (Ephesians 5:18).

The filling of the Holy Spirit is a command. The word translated into the English *be filled* is the word *plerousthe* in the original language. Every verb has a number, tense, voice, and mood. When we look at this word *be filled* in Ephesians 5:18, we find that the number is plural. The tense is present, continuous action. The voice is passive, meaning that the subject does not act. It is acted upon. The mood is imperative. There is no option. Therefore, properly translated, the command to be filled in Ephesians 5:18 is saying, "All of you must always be being filled with the Holy Spirit."

What makes a church great in the eyes of God? The first element is participation. This involves *unity* (participation with each other) and *unction* (participation with God).

What is the phenomenon of Pentecost that needs to be repeated? Is it the wind? Is it the flaming fire? Is it the *glossa* and *dialektos?* No! It is the filling! All through Acts we read repeatedly that they were filled with the Holy Spirit. That is what we need—the filling of God's Holy Spirit. At conversion we have the Holy Spirit. At the filling He has us! As they spoke in these other languages and dialects, the people heard them speaking in their own language and dialect. They spoke of the amazing wonders of God and certainly got the attention of the crowd. These tongues did not save a soul; they were attention getters. Three thousand people were saved, and the church was born when the preacher, Simon Peter, stood and preached the Lord Jesus Christ.

Revival comes through *participation* with God in the filling of His Holy Spirit. What is the real proof of being filled with God's Holy Spirit? The proof is evidenced in Ephesians 5:19-21. We will recall that the command of God is found in Ephesians 5:18, "Be filled with the Spirit." The following verse will present the *inward* evidence. That is, how will *you* know? There will be a song in your heart!

The next verse gives us the *upward* evidence. That is, how will *God* know? Of course God knows everything, but the evidence is in thankfulness. We will have a heart full of thanksgiving and praise. The *outward* evidence is in the following verse. How will *others* know? By our spirit of submission one to another.

Inward Evidence

What is the inward evidence that one is being filled with the Holy Spirit? If God's command is in Ephesians 5:18, the inward evidence is in Ephesians 5:19, "Speak to one another with psalms, hymns and spiritual songs. Sing and make music in your heart to the Lord." What is the evidence? It is singing, even if you cannot carry a tune in a bucket. This is the inward evidence of the fullness of God's Holy Spirit. We cannot stay filled with the Holy Spirit without singing. In the original text there is no period after verse 18. This is where we find the difference in Christianity and other world religions. If you look at the followers of Buddha they may have their impressive temples, but they have no song in their hearts. The Hindus may have their mantras, but they have no song in their hearts. Islam may pride itself in its morality, but they have no song in their hearts. When we are filled with the Holy Spirit, one of the sure proofs is joy. We are joyful inside. I love the title of that old song, "With a Song in My Heart." Even though we may be like Paul and Silas in a Philippian jail at midnight, we cannot help but sing. This is the *inward* evidence of a life that is filled with the Spirit of God.

Note that this inward evidence is manifested "in your heart" (Ephesians 5:19). I am so thankful that the instrument is the heart and not the vocal chords. I often sing in my car when the windows are rolled up. I cannot make melody on an instrument. I cannot make melody with my vocal chords, but I certainly can in my heart!

To whom is this inward evidence directed? "To the Lord" (Eph. 5:19). The Holy Spirit is in the world to uplift and glorify the Lord Jesus. Music is not primarily designed by God to be a tool of evangelism. In other words, Christian music should be the result of a Spirit-filled life that is pointed to God. It is not intended for the world. It is rather unfortunate that many Christian singers today dedicate their songs to the world's beat with the world's vernacular.

How is the inward evidence to be experienced? "Speaking to yourselves in psalms and hymns and spiritual

songs, singing and making melody in your heart to the Lord"
(Ephesians 5:19, KJV). Note that it is making "melody"
and not rhythm or harmony. Rhythm appeals to the body,
harmony to the soul, but melody is what appeals to the spirit.
Think about it. Whichever you find predominant in music
is where you will discover its intended appeal. I believe the
rhythm of rock music appeals to the flesh. The sentimental
harmony music appeals to the soul, the self-life. We
remember such groups as the Carpenters and all the harmony
and love songs. Melody is what appeals to the spirit. We
make melody in our hearts to the Lord. Yes, the inward
evidence of the filling of God's Holy Spirit is a song in
one's heart. If one wants to know if he or she is being filled
with the Spirit of God, this should be the first characteristic.

Upward Evidence

There is also an upward evidence of the filling of God's
Holy Spirit. "Always giving thanks to God the Father for
everything, in the name of our Lord Jesus Christ" (Eph.
5:20). Again, pay attention to whom this thanksgiving is
directed - "to God" (Eph. 5:20). When we begin to recognize
God as the Source of everything, and we allow His Spirit to
fill us, we will commence giving thanks always for all things
unto God and the Father in the name of our Lord Jesus
Christ. We are to offer this upward evidence "always."

One person chimes in, "But you do not know my
problem." Another complains, "But you do not know my
spouse." Another says, "But you do not know my situation
on the job." But the verse says, "always." We are challenged
to be thankful at all times because that attitude shows that
God is in control. Paul expressed it in these words, "Give
thanks in all circumstances, for this is God's will for you in
Christ Jesus." If we are looking for a starting point toward

finding God's will, that is precisely the place to start. There is an *inward* evidence and an *upward* evidence to the filling of God's Holy Spirit.

And notice for what we are to be thankful—"everything" (Eph. 5:20). Some are only thankful after they receive a blessing. We land a new job, and we pray, "Lord, thank you." We recover from a sickness, and we praise, "Lord, thank you." The evidence of the filling of God's Holy Spirit is that we are thankful in *all things.* This means that we must be thankful not only after our blessings, but before a blessing, in anticipation of the victory we have awareness that it will come.

Being thankful also means we are to be thankful, not merely after and before, but even in the midst of the storms of life. Jonah certainly found this truth to be liberating when he pledged, "But I, with a song of thanksgiving, will sacrifice to you. What I have vowed I will make good. Salvation comes from the Lord" (Jonah 2:9).

God appreciated that prayer of thanksgiving so much he had the fish regurgitate Jonah onto the shore. Thanksgiving, this *upward* evidence of the filling of God's Spirit, has a liberating, freeing effect. We cannot stay filled with the Holy Spirit without giving thanks always unto God for all things.

Outward Evidence

There is not only an *inward* and an *upward* evidence, but there is also an *outward* evidence of the filling of the Holy Spirit. Paul continued, "Submit to one another out of reverence for Christ" (Eph. 5:21). What is this outward evidence? It is submission. We are each to esteem the others better than ourselves. People are not sure we are filled with the Holy Spirit by our speech or the terminology we use, but the outward evidence is in our relationship with other people. Christ, of course, is our example. We remember in the upper room on the eve of His death, having instituted the Lord's Supper, how he washed his disciples' feet in a spirit of humility. Jesus was teaching all that the greatest man is one who uses His authority to build up his people and not like the Pharisees to build themselves up. The only means of showing this outward evidence to others is by being filled with the Holy Spirit.

We are to submit to "one another." This is certainly evidence of the Spirit-filled life. Here is the solution to mountains of our problems. To solve difficulties in relationships, we must come to the knowledge of the truth about ourselves. If we are filled with the Holy Spirit we readily recognize that we have nothing to boast about. A person filled with the Holy Spirit is apt to listen and learn. The Holy Spirit helps us to realize we are members of one body, and therefore, our body functions as we submit ourselves to one another. This spirit of *unity* and *unction* is the greatest factor in church growth.

The outward evidence that one is being filled with the Holy Spirit is this mutual submission—one to another. In the Ephesian letter, Paul goes on to illustrate verse 21 in three ways. The next series of verses illustrates this submission regarding the husband/wife relationship. The following verses illustrate this submission in relationship to the parent and child. And finally, to the employer and employee.

Thus, what is the proof that one is genuinely being filled with God's Holy Spirit? Is it a certain, assigned gift, or a certain terminology, or a certain miracle? No! The real proof that one is being filled with the Holy Spirit is found in the context of its command. There is an inward evidence, *a song in one's heart.* There is an upward evidence, *a spirit of thanksgiving.* There is an outward evidence, *submitting ourselves one to another.* We will never see genuine revival until each of us comes to this element of participation, not only with others in *unity* but with God in *unction,* the filling of God's Holy Spirit. This is the church member's most pressing need in these last days of church history.

Untold numbers of members in churches today try to give out when they have never taken in. Jesus declared, "He that believes in me as the Scripture has said, out of his belly will flow rivers of living water." There are two kinds of wells—surface wells and artesian wells. A surface well is not very deep.

When I was a small child, I used to visit my great-uncle who ran a country store nine miles outside Pikeville, Tennessee, on the side of a mountain. I was a city boy and quite fascinated by that life-style. They had an old water pump outside the back door of their house. He would go out and pour a little water from a Mason jar into the pump, thus "priming" the pump, and then he would pump, pump, pump, until the water started flowing. As long as he pumped, it would flow, but when he stopped so would the water. One always had to remember to fill the jar, because it would have to be primed again. Have you ever known any church members like that? If you want them to serve the Lord Jesus, you have to prime the pump. So many try to enlist workers by begging and pleading and stroking. Why? Because those people are shallow like that surface well.

However, there is another kind of well that we call an artesian well. It goes down deep into the ground until it hits an underground stream or river. You do not have to pump an artesian well, all you have to do is tap into it, and it flows and flows. I hope you have known believers like that. Those church members are not complaining, "I've been here six months, and nobody has come to see me!" They are asking, "Is there anyone I can go and visit?" These people are not carping, "No one spoke to me today!" They pick out people and make a point of speaking to them first. What is the difference? Some want to be served while others want to serve. Some are shallow, while some have tapped into the river of life and are being filled with God's Holy Spirit.

The church will be revived again when more and more of its people experience first-hand the filling of the Holy Spirit in their lives. The early church found their strength in *participation,* not only with each other, but with God: They were "all filled with the Holy Spirit."

What makes a church great in the eyes of God? The first element is vital—participation. They were all together, and they were all filled. There was unity and unction among their fellowship. They found their strength in participation with each other and participation with God. They not only had a sense of belonging to God but a sense of belonging to each other. No church will ever be a great church in the eyes of God without its membership being all together and all filled. Unity and unction are essential elements to the making of a great church in the eyes of God. What is it for you...SHIELDS OF BRASS OR SHIELDS OF GOLD?

Chapter Eight

Proclamation

There will never be a church that is a great church in the eyes of God without a bold *proclamation* of the Word of God by a God-anointed and God-appointed preacher.

Gospel proclamation became the central part of the day at Pentecost. The preaching of the Gospel should be central in the church of the Lord Jesus Christ. In the twenty-first century, it is still by the "foolishness of preaching" that people are drawn to repentance. It is not simply enough to have participation; great churches are also characterized by *proclamation.*

Prophetic

Our preaching must be prophetic. In other words, it must be biblical. Peter stood up before the crowd, raised his voice, opened the scroll to the prophet Joel, and read Joel 2:28-32. He established a scriptural basis for what was happening, and for what he desired his hearers to do in response. He then illustrated his text with Psalms 16 and 110. His preaching was prophetic and biblical. It is amazing that so many preachers do not seem to preach the Word of God today. A preacher who is not using the Bible would be as if a surgeon went into surgery without his scalpel, because preaching the Word is what "cuts to the heart" (Acts 2:37). For a preacher not to use the Word of God would be like a carpenter trying to build a home without a hammer. God spoke to us through Jeremiah saying, "Is not my word like a hammer that breaks a rock to pieces?" No wonder so many churches are empty. Our preaching must be prophetic.

The great, God-blessed churches in the world today have one common characteristic: an insistence upon an exposition of God's infallible Word. They have men behind their pulpits who select their text from the Word of God and proclaim it boldly. Peter chose a text from the prophet Joel. Joel had predicted that the Lord would come and visit His people. He prophesied that the Lord would come and live in the midst of them, and that after this supernatural visitation He would "pour out his Spirit upon all flesh." Peter asserted, "this is what was spoken by the prophet Joel" (Acts 2:16). The text was happening before their eyes.

The Bible records, "When the people heard this, they were cut to the heart" (Acts 2:37). What is it that cuts one's heart and pricks one's spirit? It is the sword, the Word of God.

The Word of God is profitable. Paul wrote to his young preacher-friend, Timothy, to remind him that "all Scripture is God-breathed and is useful for teaching, rebuking, correcting and training in righteousness, so that the man of God may be thoroughly equipped for every good work" (2 Tim. 3:16-17). The Word of God is indeed profitable. It is profitable for four things: doctrine, reproof, correction, and instruction in righteousness. An effective ministry of God's Word will do all four. It will teach doctrine, rebuke and reprove sin, correct false paths, and train and instruct in righteousness.

There are churches today that have instructed in doctrine to the virtual exclusion of instructing in righteousness or correcting false paths. These groups are dying because of their emphasis on doctrine alone.

Other churches have emphasized reproof. They feel their

God-given call is continuously to speak on how long someone's hair is or how short someone's dress is. They seldom, if ever, teach doctrine or instruct in righteousness.

There are still others who have pointed out correction to the virtual exclusion of doctrine, reproof, and instruction. Like those who have stressed reproof, they are polemic and think God has called them to correct everyone else while the lost world sits by watching and quietly going to hell.

Still others have emphasized instruction in righteousness of being Holy-Spirit filled to the virtual exclusion of ever teaching doctrine. This constant emphasis on the deeper life without any strong doctrinal teaching, preaching, reproof, or correction has led to more than one division in the local body of believers.

An effective ministry of God's Word will be a balanced ministry and will do all four vital things. The Bible is profitable when it is used in a prophetic sense. As we look at Simon Peter's sermon, we find all four of these elements included. He taught doctrine as he spoke of the Deity of Christ (Acts 2:31-33,36). He reproved sin (Acts 2:23). He corrected false paths and instructed in righteousness (Acts 2:38). Peter preached a balanced, biblical, prophetic message.

First, the proclamation of the gospel must be prophetic. The only way it can be prophetic is to be biblical. What makes a church great in the eyes of God? Participation and proclamation, Bible preaching is prophetic.

Plain

Second, it must also be plain. In Acts 2:14, Peter proclaimed, "Let me explain this to you; listen carefully to what I say." He was being *plain* in his approach. Peter did not make it difficult; he simply laid out the plain truth of the Word of God. He preached about sin, God's mercy in Christ, and the coming judgment, and the common people understood him. Many preachers today make their message difficult to understand. This gospel, of which we are stewards, is plain enough for a child to understand. Many churches never make an impact, because they do not preach the plain gospel. People can attend some churches for months (maybe even years) and never know what they must do to have eternal life.

The first Christian sermon was Christ-centered. Peter preached of Christ. He preached about Jesus in His incarnation, death, resurrection, and presence by His Spirit. Peter did not preach systematic theology nor philosophy, he preached Jesus: He was born to save, died on the cross, arose again, ascended, and is coming again. Peter was *plain* in his approach. He sent the message home:

> *"This man was handed over to you by God's set purpose and foreknowledge; and you, with the help of wicked men, put him to death by nailing him to the cross" (Acts 2:23).*

Who crucified our Lord? The Jews? The Romans? No! I did, and you did—my sin, your sin. But in the truest sense—God did! No one took our Lord's life; He laid it down.

Peter was *plain* in the message of the gospel. The transparent truth is that the cross was no accident. Some people think the cross was some sort of last-minute band-aid on a wounded world when everything else had failed. No! A thousand times, no!

It was the program and plan of God. Peter continued in Acts 2:23: "This man was handed over to you by God's set purpose and foreknowledge." The word translated *purpose* in the *New International Version* of the Bible is the Greek word *boule.* It means God's irrevocable will, which will be done with or without our cooperation or response.

There is another word, when translated, that is the English word *counsel (purpose* or *will)* which in Greek is *thelema,* simply meaning desire. We do not find that word in Acts 2:23. Instead, we discover the stronger word *boule.*

Therefore, what Peter was preaching to the crowd is this: There is nothing you could do that could have stopped or altered God's plan for the atonement of our sins at Calvary! God was in control. The Lord Jesus was handed over to you by God's "boule," God's irrevocable will, which was to be done with or without our cooperation or consent. Peter's message was plain. He preached Jesus. What makes a great church? It must have the element of proclamation, which is prophetic and plain.

Positive

Third, proclamation must also be positive. Peter continued: "God has raised this Jesus to life, and we are all witnesses of the fact" (Acts 2:32). Peter unfurled the resurrection. The resurrection should be the heart of every sermon. Our Lord is not dead. He is alive! He is here and can meet our needs today. We have a *positive* gospel!

These disciples had seen the resurrected Christ, and He had transformed their lives. Most of them met martyrs' deaths. If they had been perpetrating a lie, they would not have died for their faith. Persons do not die for a lie. Peter was crucified upside-down in Rome. Being a martyr was one of the most marvelous proofs of the resurrection. Peter had seen the risen Lord. Jesus was alive! The resurrection should inject a positive note into our preaching, not some sort of superficial, pumped-up mental attitude. Every preacher should ask himself how much of his preaching points to the living Christ.

So many of our congregations today argue, "I have to see it, and then I will believe it."

But God says just the opposite, "You believe it, and then you will see it."

Remember Thomas in the upper room? He struggled about this point, "I will have to see it; then I will believe it." Jesus, appearing in His resurrected body, left this with him, "Thomas, blessed are those who have not seen and yet have believed." Where can we gain our positive spirit in preaching? We do not receive it from positive thinking or from possibility thinking. We should gather it from the same event Peter did, and that is the resurrection. The Lord Jesus is alive, and therefore our proclamation should be positive. There is not a need in the heart of any hearer that the living Christ cannot meet!

It was a hot, June day in Ada, Oklahoma. Early that morning I was pacing the second floor corridor at Valley View Hospital. It was a special day for our family, as our little Holly was making her grand entrance into our world. It was not long until Dr. Stevens appeared in the nursery windows and held that tiny package of love, wrapped in a pink blanket. He laid her in a bassinet and wheeled her over to the window where I could have a good look. Only a daddy can know the joy of that moment. I stood there alone for several minutes, thanking the Lord and watching that little, red-faced beauty waving her arms, kicking her feet, and crying at the top of her lungs.

Suddenly, I noticed I was no longer standing there alone. A housekeeper with her mop bucket was looking over my shoulder. "Is that your baby?" she asked.

"Surely is," I proudly answered.

She continued, "Well, it's no wonder she is crying, being

born into the world she has been born into." She turned around and sauntered down the hall, pushing her mop bucket before her.

For a moment I began to think, she is right. If I believe everything I preach and teach, then it would be far better for this little girl to go on to heaven. After all, she would not have to go through all the heartaches of life and never have the haunting longing that some moment could be lived over.

I began to pray. It was an intimate moment with Jesus, Holly, and me. I often pray hymns in my private devotional time, and that morning the Holy Spirit began to pray, through me, the words of a Bill Gaither hymn, "Because He Lives." When I began the second verse of the hymn, I knew I was on holy ground:

How sweet to hold a new born baby,
And feel the pride, and joys she gives;
But greater still the calm assurance,
This child can face uncertain days because he
lives.
Because he lives I can face tomorrow;
Because he lives, all fear is gone;
Because I know he holds the future,
And life is worth the living
Just because he lives.

What makes a church great in the eyes of God? It is not only made up of participation, but also *proclamation.* Our proclamation must be *prophetic, plain,* and *positive.*

Personal

Fourth, proclamation must also be personal. Although Peter was preaching to a multitude of people, he was preaching on a personal level. Hear him as he says, "This man was handed over to *you* by God's set purpose and foreknowledge; and *you,* with the help of wicked men, put *him* to death by nailing *him* to the cross" (Acts 2:23, author's italics). Note the personal pronouns. Preaching today is mostly in the first person plural or the third person plural. That is, we are told to use a lot of *we* and *they* in our preaching. This type of preaching seldom brings about conviction.

Peter preached in second person, saying, "You, with the help of wicked men, put him to death by nailing him to the cross." You, you, you!

There are many preachers today who are afraid of offending deacons, elders, vestrymen, big givers, this person or that person, that civic leader or politician. It is no wonder many churches today have such little power. Our proclamation should be personal. Peter's preaching was not aimed just at the head but also at the heart. It was personal, and when he finished, the Bible reports, "When the people heard this, they were cut to the heart" (Acts 2:37).

What makes a church great in the eyes of God? The element of proclamation is vital. This proclamation must not only be *prophetic, plain,* and *positive,* it must also be *personal.*

Penetrating

Fifth, it must also be penetrating. Acts 2:37 tells us, "When the people heard this, they were cut to the heart and said to Peter and the other apostles, "Brothers, what shall we do?" What happened? The Word testifies that the people's hearts were "cut." We have a word for that; we call it conviction. Much modern preaching is superficial, designed to make the hearers feel good. I have heard preachers in some churches even boast that people can come to their services and never feel guilty about their lifestyles. They advertise that they are there to "make you feel good." Well, Peter's sermon "cut his hearers to the heart." The truth is, the only way we will ever feel good about ourselves is to see ourselves for who we are, to confess that our sin put Christ on the cross. Once we realize this and are set free through the blood of Jesus Christ, we will have the best feeling we have ever had. Then we will be able to sing:

Free from the law, Oh happy condition
Jesus bled and there is remission
Cursed by the fall, condemned by the law
Christ has redeemed us, once for all.
Lyrics by P. P. BLISS

Until a person sees that there is no hope within himself to satisfy the righteous demands of the law, the cross is simply a farce to him. When conviction of sin arrives, we are aware that the only way we can get right with God is through the cross of our Lord Jesus Christ. Some people have never felt conviction. Their hearts have never been cut. Why? Because in too many cases they have not been under the preaching of the gospel that is prophetic, plain, positive, and personal.

When these men and women at Pentecost realized what they had done in crucifying the Lord Jesus Christ, their hearts were broken. Why aren't more people's hearts cut in our churches today? It is because they do not realize that they ought to assume personal responsibility for their sin. And why? Because there is not enough preaching today that is penetrating. There are few preachers who even mention sin today. Sin is often the forgotten word in the pulpit today. No wonder many churches are dead and dying. There is no conviction in them, and without conviction there can be no conversion!

Conviction always precedes conversion. These people were "cut to the heart." This was a recognition of sin. Here is a broken and contrite heart. This process is called spiritual birth, and it is pictured in physical birth. There must be birth pains before the child is born, and so it is in spiritual birth. We cannot experience the new birth without godly sorrow over sin any more than one can give natural childbirth without experiencing birth pains. Conviction leads to conversion. A host of people make some sort of "decision" early in life but have never really realized that they have personally sinned and put Christ on the cross. They were never really "cut to the heart" because of their sin.

Here we find the first account of the convicting work of the Holy Spirit. Jesus had prophesied the night before the crucifixion, "But I tell you the truth: It is for your good that I am going away. Unless I go away, the Counselor will not come to you; But if I go, I will send him to you. When he comes, he will convict the world of guilt in regard to sin and righteousness and judgment: in regard to sin, because men do not believe in me" (John 16:7-9).

While in my first pastorate at Hobart, Oklahoma, I learned a lot from those southwestern Oklahoma wheat farmers. I learned as much from those dear, old individuals who had spent a lifetime in the Book of God than I did from some of my professors. Being a city boy, I was fascinated by farm life. I learned there were several things necessary in order to grow a good crop.

First, the ground had to be broken. Farmers would use their tractors and plows and turn the sod over and over, breaking up the dirt. Second, the seed had to be planted. Third, the wheat was cultivated, watered, and nurtured. Finally, about the first of June every year, the harvest was gathered!

Many churches today wonder why they never reap a harvest. Perhaps they have never broken ground! The Word of God cuts to the heart, and often there is not a great deal of preaching regarding the Word of God. Our preaching must be penetrating. We will never see the harvest if we do not preach the Word of God. It does not matter whether the seed is planted or whether the ground is cultivated, if it is not first broken, there will be no harvest.

What makes a church great? The element of participation and the element of proclamation. Our proclamation should be *prophetic, plain, personal* and *penetrating.*

Persuasive

Sixth, it must also be persuasive. Acts 2:37 says, "When the people heard this, they were cut to the heart and said to Peter and the other apostles, "Brothers, what shall we do?". God-anointed preaching is *persuasive* preaching. It goes straight to the heart, and people begin to ask what was asked in this text, "What shall we do?" What a question! One who is convicted does not know what to do. It is not in the natural man's heart. It is "not by works of righteousness which we have done, but according to his mercy he has saved us" (Titus 3:5, KJV).

Much preaching today falls on deaf ears, and often it is not the hearer's fault. At least many hearers are there, in their place and in their pew. Much of the preaching today is not persuasive, because in place of being plain it is complicated; in place of being positive it is critical; in place of being personal it is courteous, so as not to offend; and in place of being penetrating it is often cosmetic. No wonder modern preaching is not leading more people to ask, "What shall we do?"

What shall we do? This is the basic question we must ask in the twenty-first century church if Jesus tarries. What shall we do? It is not enough to be sorry for our sin. What shall we do? The question has a real ring of desperation in it. What shall we do? It is like the Philippian jailer who asked, "What must I do to be saved?" (Acts 16:30).

On the Day of Pentecost the hearers were "cut to the heart" (Acts 2:37). Note when they asked the question, "What shall we do?" It was when they heard Peter say in the previous verse, "God has made this Jesus whom you crucified both Lord and Christ." Jesus is Lord! He is risen from the dead, and He is Lord. This confronts us all with the question, "What shall we do?" What shall we do about the Lordship of Jesus Christ? Josh McDowell says he is either Lord or liar, and our eternal destiny hinges upon what we believe about this fact.

If the church in America today had sufficient power, today's masses, as the crowd did at Pentecost, would first be asking, "What does this mean?" (Acts 2:12). Then they would be asking, "What shall we do?" (Acts 2:37). Our proclamation must be persuasive.

Pointed

Seventh, it must also be pointed. Peter answered their question with a pointed reply by saying, "repent" (Acts 2:38). He told his hearers what they ought to do. He did not give them several multiple-choice options. He was pointed. In a word he replied, "repent." What shall we do? Repent. Much preaching today is so vague. People can sit in some churches for months without any idea of how to apply the message to their lives on Monday through Friday. Preaching must not only be prophetic, it must be *pointed*.

Peter's pointed proclamation was a word—repent. There are three pertinent questions to be asked at this point: *What is repentance? Why is repentance important? And where is repentance found in the salvation process?*

First, what is repentance? There seems to be considerable confusion regarding what repentance is. Let's look first at what repentance is *not*. Repentance is not *remorse.* It is not simply being sorry for our sin. Remorse may lead to repentance, but remorse is not repentance. The rich, young ruler went away very sorrowful when Jesus explained the demands of discipleship. He was remorseful, but he did not repent. Many people have substituted remorse for repentance.

Repentance is not *regret.* That is, it is not merely wishing some sinful deed, word, or action had not occurred. Pontius Pilate ceremonially took a basin of water and washed his hands, regretting his evil deed, but he did not repent. Many people substitute regret for repentance and tragically fool themselves in the process.

Repentance is not *resolve.* All of us have made New Year's resolutions. Many of us resolve to assume a new set of moral standards and live life on a higher plane but never seem able to turn that "new leaf over" for any considerable period of time. We cannot substitute resolve for repentance.

It is not enough to sing "I Am Resolved," unless that is coupled with "godly sorrow," unless the repentance is genuine within one's heart, and unless there is a determination wrought by the Holy Spirit, in which one never wants to sin again, even though such is impossible here. But there must be that determination none the less. Genuine repentance is characterized by the person's saying to himself and God, "I never want to displease the Lord again. I am so sorry for my sins. I am leaving that old life behind me. I don't want to be the same. I want to be changed by the Holy Spirit."

Through the years, I have heard many people make resolves that they have never followed. They bargained with the Lord, "0, Lord, if you just get me out of this mess, I'll do whatever You want. I'll follow wherever you lead. Lord, just help me." And the Lord does help them. They get out of their jam. They go on living as they did before, making a mockery out of God, ignoring Him, and never looking back to those resolutions, because they were not accompanied by real repentance and doing an about-face from sin. A mere resolution will not suffice.

Repentance is not *reform*. Sometimes reformation even involves restitution. It was so with Judas Iscariot. After betraying our Lord, he grabbed the thirty pieces of silver, returned to the temple and threw it at those who had paid the price of betrayal. Judas reformed, but unfortunately he did not repent. Many people today have substituted reform for repentance. Peter did not preach on the Day of Pentecost and say, "Reform." Nor did he say, "Resolve." Nor did he say, "Regret." Nor did he say, "Have remorse." His message was a pointed call for repentance.

We have seen what repentance is not; now let us examine what repentance is. Is repentance turning from every sin as some people preach today? If so, then who has repented? When you came to Christ, did you turn from every sin you had ever committed? The truth is, in our natural state we are spiritually dead, not sick, and therefore unresponsive to the gospel. The Bible reminds us: "The natural man receiveth not the things of the Spirit of God: for they are foolishness to him: neither can he know them, because they are spiritually discerned" (1 Cor. 2:14, KJV). What is repentance? The word *repent* is the Greek word *metanoia,* which in its original language is defined as a change of mind. It is to change one's way of thinking about salvation. Repentance makes you love what you once hated, and hate what you once loved. When I was converted at age seventeen, I had never heard the word *repentance*. It was weeks or perhaps months after my conversion before I ever remember hearing the word. I know I repented! How do I know? The bad things I used to love, I no longer desired, and the things I never thought I would like became the things I loved to do. It was a change of mind.

Repentance is a change of mind. Repentance involves a change of your mind about yourself, a change of your mind about sin, and a change of your mind about salvation. It is a change of mind that is always evidenced in three areas.

First, *attitude* is changed intellectually. As stated, it is a change of mind. This is where we begin. This is repentance.

Second, there is a change in the *affections of the* heart. If one genuinely changes one's mind, then a change of heart will follow.

The third result of a change of mind is a change in *action*. There will be a change in one's will or volition. If we genuinely changed our minds, our hearts will be changed, and if our hearts have been changed, a change in our will, will follow. Paul said, "Therefore, if anyone is in Christ, he is a new creation; the old has gone, the new has come!" (2 Cor. 5:17). If we have experienced salvation our lives will be altered. We will no longer look at life, ourselves, and others as we once did. Like the prodigal son, God will give us new wishes and desires. This is repentance!

Since repentance is a change of mind, a person may be moved to tears emotionally by a sermon, and one's heart may overflow with remorse or regret, but it is not necessarily repentance. A person may have one's will manipulated by various means, but if he or she has not repented (changed one's mind), he or she is not saved. Jesus made it clear, "Except ye repent, ye shall all likewise perish" (Luke 13:3, KJV).

We find our most obvious biblical illustration of repentance in Luke 15 with the story of the prodigal son. Here was a young man who had gone to a far country and wasted all of his inheritance on ungodly living. He was far away from home. First of all, this boy came to have *a change of attitude.* Luke 15:17 (KJV) notes "he came to himself" that is, he changed his mind. Then what happened? He had *a change of affection.* He thought to himself,

> *"How many hired servants have bread enough and to spare, and I am perishing with hunger! I will arise and go to my father, and will say unto him, Father, I have sinned against heaven, and before thee, And am no longer worthy to be called thy son" (Luke 15:17-19, KJV).*

His heart was changed. Then what happened after his change of mind resulted in a changed heart? He had *a change of action;* his will was changed, and so was his direction. "I will arise and go to my father." And Luke 15:20 states: "He got up and went to his father."

The prodigal son had a change of mind. That was repentance. It was evident in four areas. He regretted his deed; he blamed himself for his sin; he acknowledged his father's right to be displeased, as he felt he was no longer worthy to be called his father's son; and he resolved to sin no more. After this, he went home. Repentance is a change of mind. The battle is in the mind, and the proof is in these four areas. Each of us will repent when we change our minds, and in changing our minds, our hearts will be changed. Therefore, a change in our will and volition will follow. This change of mind will cause us to regret our deed and blame ourselves for it, take responsibility for the deed, and resolve to set our face toward the Lord Jesus Christ.

By now it should be apparent why repentance is important. To begin with, it was the message of the Old Testament prophets, who were all preachers of repentance. As far back as Noah, we hear them calling on the people to forsake their wicked ways and turn to the Lord.

It was the message of the forerunner John the Baptist: "Repent, for the kingdom of heaven is near" (Matt. 3:2). And Matthew 3:7-8 says, "But when he saw many of the Pharisees and Sadducees coming to where he was baptizing, he said to them; "You brood of vipers. Who warned you to flee from the coming wrath? Produce fruit in keeping with repentance."

Let's face it. I doubt if John the Baptist could make it as a pastor in most churches today. His preaching was pointed. He preached without fear or favor. He laid the ax to the tree. He did not care who it offended, if God laid the message on his heart.

John the Baptist denounced Herod for adultery. He referred to his listeners as vipers and snakes. How long would a preacher last, if he called his listeners snakes, unless he was preaching to real snakes the kind that slither and have forked tongues? And what kind of response did he receive? The common people rejoiced over his straightforward ministry. However, the folks at the palace did not like him. Herodias asked Herod for John's (decapitated) head on a platter in exchange for an exotic dance from Salome. John the Baptist was imprisoned and then beheaded for preaching the truth pointedly.

It was the message of the Lord Jesus Himself. He commenced His ministry with the message of repentance. The Bible reports, "From that time on Jesus began to preach "Repent, for the kingdom of heaven is near" (Matthew. 4:17). In Mark 1:14-15: After John was put in prison, Jesus went into Galilee, proclaiming the good news of God. "The time has come," he said. "The kingdom of God is near. Repent and believe the good news!"

Jesus continued His ministry with the message of repentance by saying, "I tell you, no! But unless you repent, you too will all perish" (Luke 13:3). The burden of His heart was, in a word *repent.* Jesus concluded His ministry with the word *repentance* as recorded in Luke 24:46-47: He told them, "This is what is written: The Christ will suffer and rise from the dead on the third day, and repentance and forgiveness of sins will be preached in his name in all nations."

Jesus' first sermon was "Repent and believe the good news." It was also the message of the Great Commission. In Matthew's account of this, God gives us the mechanics. We are to *make* disciples, *mark* disciples by baptism, and *mature* disciples by teaching them to observe the faith. These are the *mechanics* of the Great Commission, and Mark's account gives us the *measure* of it.

We are commanded to take the gospel to the whole world. Luke's account of the Commission gives us the message of the Great Commission. What is it? "That repentance and remission of sins should be preached... among all nations" (Luke 24:47, KJV). Jesus *commenced, continued,* and *concluded* His ministry with the same word, *repent.* How can a minister today claim to be preaching the gospel of Jesus Christ if he leaves out the heart of our Lord's message? *Our preaching must be pointed.*

It was also the message of the apostles. "They went out and preached that people should repent" (Mark 6:12). They went out and preached. What did they preach? Prosperity? Successful living? What? They went out and preached that people should repent.

It was the message of Simon Peter. Hear him at Pentecost, raising his voice in his mighty sermon, and answering the question of what the people should do with a one-word reply "Repent!"

It was the message of the apostle Paul. Hear him: "In the past God overlooked such ignorance, but now he commands all people everywhere to repent"'(Acts 17:30). Hear him later: "I have declared to both Jews and Greeks that they must turn to God in repentance and have faith in our Lord Jesus" (Acts 20:21).

It was the message of John the beloved apostle. Simply turn to the message directed to the churches of Asia, as recorded in the early chapters of Revelation, and discover that eight times, in letters to the seven churches, he pealed forth the message of repentance. Why is it important? Because it is the message of the Bible.

What was the message of the Bible? What was the message of the early church? Was it positive thinking, with all sorts of trinkets for reminders? Was it concentrated ministries on the home, ministries on finance, or selected other "professional ministries"? When we read the Book of Acts, we find none of these in the early church. Why? Their message was "repent."

This is what accounts for a happy home when a husband and wife repent. We can fill out workbooks until we are blue in the face and sit before videotaped seminars until we can sit no longer (and some of those are good), but I believe what the church severely needs today is the message of repentance. When a person genuinely repents, he or she will put one's home in order.

It is strange how many preachers are silent today concerning the message of repentance. It could be that some have lost sight of the sinfulness of humankind. Today some are preaching who deny the Bible truth of a literal, burning hell, or at least they never mention it. There are many preachers today who hold the doctrine of universalism, believing that ultimately and eventually everyone will be saved. Consequently, what need is there for the message of repentance in these churches? Too many churches and preachers have lost sight of the lostness of humankind and the holiness of God. Perhaps it is because repentance is not a popular message. Of course, it is indeed more popular to "tickle the ears" of our listeners with messages of comfort, sweetness, and light.

There is a positive motive that produces repentance. It is not so much the message of "bumper-sticker evangelism" which might read, "Turn or burn." It is more the message found in the Roman letter where Paul says, "God's kindness [goodness] leads you toward repentance" (Romans 2:4).

We are so privileged to hear the gospel: The gospel which millions (perhaps billions) of people on our planet have never heard. We are privileged to take them the message of repentance. Today, missionaries' feet have never before walked in so many little villages. A copy of God's Word has not been translated into the dialects and languages of some, and they die in the darkness; millions going down. And us? We are placed in the very spotlight of the Christian life. And yet, few of us have any time for the Lord Jesus. Can't we understand that it is the goodness of God which allows us to hear the gospel and that this is what lcads us to repentance? Peter stood up and shouted, "Repent!"

The Bible does not indicate that it is the kindness of God that *calls* us to repentance, but it says, "The kindness of God *leads* us to repentance." The truth is God calls us to repentance by the gospel, but God leads us to repentance by His goodness. The goodness of God comes to us where we are; takes us by the hand, as though we were a little child; and leads us to repentance. The goodness of God leads us to repentance.

His amazing grace is offered freely through His goodness and mercy. He guides and leads the unconverted person toward repentance, God, faith, and our Lord Jesus Christ (Acts 21:20). Many are the questions which frail humans raise.

Doubters and others who have grown bitter remind me of an illustration I heard years ago. You see, the goodness, kindness, and love of God are like the sun. We could compare the heart to butter or mud. When the sun beats down on the butter, it melts. When the sun shines on the mud, it turns hard like brick. This is the nature of the human heart.

When the convicting Son of God shines upon some hearts, they melt like butter. When He beams upon other hearts, they turn to hardened brick. Only the goodness of God can lead us to repentance, and men and women must let Him do His work of repentance.

When our children were little my family and I would spend vacations in a quaint little village in the Great Smoky Mountains known as Maggie Valley. It is a refreshing retreat, far from the massive traffic jams and bustle of the big city. It is like stepping into a time tunnel; there are sights and sounds that we never see and hear in our metropolis.

One summer, when our girls were small, we rented an old, white farmhouse on the side of a mountain. It was a lovely spot, but a little scary for our two small, city girls. The children slept upstairs, and the whole house creaked whenever anyone took a step. The first night happened to be one of those pitch black summer nights in the mountains. As James Weldon Johnson described in *God's Trombones,* "It was blacker than a hundred midnights down in a cypress swamp."

I was awakened in the middle of the night by the cries of our youngest daughter, who was only six or seven years old at the time. I bounded up the stairs to find her standing in the dark, calling for me. Taking her by the hand, I led her down the steps into the security of my bed where she slept soundly for the rest of the night. And so, our dear Heavenly Father finds us in the dark and takes us by the hand. The Bible gives a comforting word, "The kindness of God leads us to repentance."(Romans 2:4). When these men and women at Pentecost asked, "What shall we do?" Peter's reply came quickly. "Repent!" What should we do in our twentieth-century world? The Bible answers us plainly and clearly. Repent! Change your mind. Turn around. Go in a different direction.

So what is the message the church should be preaching today? Repentance. Peter was preaching: "You have missed God's offer of salvation. You are missing the purpose for which you were created."

What can you do about it? Change your mind! Change your mind about your sin. Change your mind about the Lord Jesus Christ. Change your mind about yourself. Change your mind about the plan of salvation. Note Peter's promise is that they would receive forgiveness. He did not promise them wind, fire, or tongues. The important aspect here is forgiveness of sin.

God-anointed preaching produces *conviction.* This leads

to *conversion* and then to *confession.* This is the order. It begins with conviction (Acts 2:37), which leads to conversion and results in confession (Acts 2:38). Baptism is vitally important, not for conversion but for confession. It signifies outwardly what has occurred inwardly. Our preaching must be pointed. It must tell people what the text says and what it wants them to do. The Christian's primary desire should always be to win people to repentance toward God and faith in the Lord Jesus Christ. What makes a great church in the eyes of God? There has never been a great church in the eyes of God that did not make much of a proclamation that was prophetic, plain, positive, personal, penetrating, persuasive, and pointed.

Pious

Eighth, it must also be pious. By pious we mean "God fearing." We are not talking about piety in the sense of its modern connotation, but pious in the sense that we fear God and realize that He is the sovereign Lord. That is what Peter meant when he used the phrase "all whom the Lord our God will call" (Acts 2:39). Our proclamation must be pious. Anointed preachers and teachers realize that God is sovereign and that He is the one who adds to the church; thus they have a real sense of dependence upon Him and a deeper desire to be faithful to His Word in life and lip. Acts 2:39 is a key to understanding this vital principle. "The promise is for you and your children and for all who are far off—for all whom the Lord our God will call." The promise is for all whom our Lord God will call. There are two types of calls—the outward call and the inward call. Peter gave the outward call, but do you know who was saved that day? Not everyone there was saved. In fact, the Bible tells us that some of them mocked him. The ones who were saved that day were "all whom the Lord God called." Our proclamation must be pious in that we realize our job is faithfulness to the outward call and trust in the Lord Jesus by His Spirit to issue the inward call.

Through the years many people who have rejected the Lord have alibied to me, "Well, preacher, I just do not want to become a Christian now, but I will later, when I feel like the time is right." I have pointed out that you cannot come to Jesus at your convenience. It has to be in *His time*. It must be when He calls.

This is why evangelists like Billy Graham have preached, in essence, so many times, "If you have the slightest impulse to come to Jesus Christ, do it now, because God has put that call into your heart. It may not come tomorrow."

"Now is the accepted time; behold, now is the day of salvation" (2 Cor. 6:2, KJV). That means the day of salvation is when God gives that inward call. For you to be truly saved, the Holy Spirit must be dealing with your heart. You must be under conviction.

In many churches today, the conviction of the Holy Spirit is never preached. Where there is no conviction, there can be no salvation. The apostle John in his Gospel quoted Jesus Himself as He prepared the apostles for His crucifixion, resurrection, and His ascension.

> *"I will not leave you comfortless: I will come to you" (14:18, KJV).*

> *And when he [Holy Spirit] is come, he will reprove the world of sin, and of righteousness, and of judgment: Of sin, because they believe not on me, Of righteousness, because I go to my Father, and ye see me no more; Of judgment, because the prince of this world is judged" (16:8-11, KJV).*

Who does the convicting? The Holy Spirit. Who does the convincing and converting? The Holy Spirit. And without convicting power working in one's life, you can never be saved.

As you read the lines, and you sense that you are unsaved, hope with all of your heart that you will fall under conviction, that you will see your sins that have sent Jesus to the cross, and that you will see yourself as God presently sees you-undone, condemned, lost, but also as precious in His sight. Long for the conviction that will lead to your repentance and faith.

Consider the following words of our Lord at this very point:

> *"All that the Father gives me will come to me, and whoever comes to me I will never drive away" (John 6:37).*

> *"No one can come to me unless the Father who sent me draws him, and I will raise him up at the last day" (John 6:44).*

Do you remember Jesus' declaration to Simon Peter after Peter's great confession at Caesarea Philippi? "Blessed are you, Simon son of Jonah, for this was not revealed to you by man, but by my Father in heaven"(Matthew. 16:17).

Paul put it like this:

> *"Because those who are led by the Spirit of God are sons of God." (Romans. 8:14).*

> *But when God, who set me apart from birth and called me by his grace, was pleased (Galatians 1:15).*

> *Peter declared, "But you are a chosen people, a royal priesthood, a holy nation, a people belonging to God, that you may declare the praises of him who called you out of darkness into*

his wonderful light." (1 Peter 2:9).
"And the God of all grace, who called you to his
eternal glory in Christ, after you have suffered a
little while, will himself restore you and make you
strong, firm and steadfast." (1 Peter 5:10).

How can two people sit on the same pew in the same worship service, sing the same songs, hear the same sermon with the same anointing, and one of them feel absolutely no need of coming to Christ or anything spiritual for that matter in his heart, and the other fall under deep conviction of sin and a longing to know Jesus personally? How can this happen? It happens by the inward call of God.

The most obvious Scripture illustration of this point is found in Acts 16, when Paul was preaching at the riverside near Philippi. The Bible records, One of those listening was a woman named Lydia, a dealer in purple cloth from the city of Thyatira, who was a worshiper of God. *The Lord opened her heart* to respond to Paul's message (Acts 16:14, author's italics).

Paul issued the outward call, and the Lord spoke to Lydia's heart, issuing the inward call.

There are a few extremists today who have carried these doctrines of grace to the point of perverting the Scripture by denying the free offer of the gospel, and in so doing have set their camps dangerously close to the border of heresy. The fact that salvation is God's work, and He takes the initiative in calling us, does not diminish one's intensity in preaching the gospel to every creature and sharing the outward call to every last person on this planet. We have a Great Commission to "preach the gospel to every creature" (Mark 16:15, KJV). This is why doctrines of grace should intensify our evangelistic efforts. We are to proclaim to the world the outward call and then trust the Holy Spirit to issue the inward call. Here again is this element of the participation of God in the call of the gospel.

The Spirit and the bride say, "Come!" And let him who hears say, "Come!" Whoever is thirsty, let him come; and whoever wishes, let him take the free gift of the water of life (Rev. 22:17).

Here we see the outward call and the inward call. The bride (the church of Jesus Christ) says come—this is the outward call. There is also the inward call—the Spirit says come. What makes a great church? It must be a church that proclaims the Word of God in a sense that is totally dependent upon the Holy Spirit.

> *Rescue the perishing,*
> *Care for the dying,*
> *Snatch them in pity*
> *from sin and the grave;*
> *Weep o'er the erring one, Lift up the fallen,*
> *Tell them of Jesus the mighty to save.*
> *Rescue the perishing,*
> *Care for the dying; Jesus is merciful,*
> *Jesus will save.*
> Lyrics by FANNIE J. CROSBY

Persistent

Ninth, it must also be persistent. The Bible says, "With many other words. . . he pleaded with them" (Acts 2:40). The English word translated *pleading* or *exhorting* is the word *parakeleo.* It means to beseech with strong force, to call forth. It is a calling to one side. Peter did not preach, sit down, cross his legs, and look humble. He did not preach and say, "Now let's sing a hymn, and if by chance anyone might possibly want to step forward for Christ, you can do so at this time, but please do not feel like you have to."

Peter did not apologize. What did he do? He gave a gospel invitation. When he finished with his sermon, he pleaded for souls. "With many other words he pleaded with them."

There should always be an appeal *after* the gospel is preached. The reverse is also true. The gospel should always be preached *before* an appeal is given. We should never issue an appeal until after the gospel is preached.

Many of us have heard evangelists who tell one deathbed story after another, moving on the emotions of the hearers, never having within their message the "kerygma" the fact that He who knew no sin became sin for us that we might become the righteousness of God in Him. There is considerable fall-out of "new converts" due to this. Peter preached the gospel and then made an appeal; such is biblical and right. He pleaded for souls that day. He exhorted them. "With many words" he besought them with strong force to receive Christ.

He pleaded with them to "save yourselves from this corrupt generation." Although God takes the initiative, God *chooses, calls, convicts,* and *converts,* and *we* must *confess.* We must identify with the Lord Jesus Christ. Paul said it this way, "For with the heart man believeth unto righteousness; and with the mouth confession is made unto salvation" (Rom. 10:10, KJV). Peter was calling for a decision. "With many other words he warned them; and he pleaded with them, "Save yourselves from this corrupt generation"(Acts 2:40).

For the true preacher of the gospel, preaching is not a profession; it is an obsession. In a sense, that is true for every believer. Every waking minute it is a part of our lives. Our proclamation must be *persistent.* There is a note of urgency here. What makes a church great in the eyes of God? The element of *participation* and also the element of *proclamation.* Our preaching must be *prophetic, plain, positive, penetrating, persuasive, pointed, pious,* and *persistent.*

Productive

Tenth, it must also be productive. Acts 2:41 reported, "Those who accepted his message were baptized, and about three thousand were added to their number that day." Three thousand precious persons were saved that day and followed the Lord in believer's baptism. It is apparent that the Bible does not contain a word about these newly baptized believers speaking in *glossa.* Although Acts 2:38 shows, "You will receive the gift of the Holy Spirit."

No doubt most of those converts at Pentecost were Jews. So far as we know, the first church was largely made up of Jews. It is wrong to think that all the Jews in the first century rejected the Christian religion. No! They were the first ones who really accepted Him. They accepted all that the prophets had foretold about the Messiah, and many saw Him as Jesus of Nazareth.

The truth about the Christian church is we do not ask Jewish people to convert to our religion; we have converted to theirs. The Lord Jesus is indeed the Jewish Messiah. Had you visited the first church in Jerusalem (30 AD), you would have found it composed almost totally of Jewish believers.

Three thousand people were saved in one day! They did so much with so little, and we seem to do so little with so much! What a gorgeous picture here of Christ receiving sinners. He casts out none who trust in Him.

What makes a church great? The element of *participation* which involves unity and unction is vitally important. There has never been a great church in the eyes

of God that did not make much Bible *proclamation* which was *prophetic, plain, positive, personal, penetrating, persuasive, pointed, pious, persistent,* and *productive.*

Chapter Nine

Preservation

*Those who accepted his message were baptized,
and about three thousand were added to their
number that day.
They devoted themselves to the apostles' teaching
and to the fellowship, to the breaking of bread and
to prayer. Everyone was filled with awe, and
many wonders and miraculous signs were done by
the apostles. All the believers were together and
had everything in common.
Selling their possessions and goods, they gave to
anyone as he had need. Every day they continued
to meet together in the temple courts. They broke
bread in their homes and ate together with glad
and sincere hearts (Acts 2:41-46).*

Great churches are not only made up of *participation*
and *proclamation* but also *preservation.* The Bible says
these early believers "devoted themselves" (Acts 2:42) and
that they "continued steadfastly" (Acts 2:42, KJV). There
are three elements involved in the *preservation* of new
converts in the church of Jesus Christ. They are *baptism,*
the *Bible,* and *body life.*

One can never grow to Christian maturity apart from
the Bible. Perhaps the worst problem in many churches is
a host of spiritual infants who have never grown in their
faith.

Two eight-year-old boys were brought to Orlando to

their world-famous amusement parks. They each had a disease which aged their bodies far in advance of their years. While the boys were only children, their appearance was that of eighty-year-old men. They were children who had grown old and were about to die but had never grown up.

As I watched those two boys on the newscast, I thought about how so many are like that in the church today. They are children who have grown old in the faith but have never grown up. This is a tragedy of today's church.

If you have ever had a baby in your home, there are some things you have readily observed. As much as you love them, babies do want their own way. They want what they want, when they want it! Also, you will note that babies seem basically lazy. That is, they lie around a lot.

They do not (and cannot) wash any of the dishes, make any of the beds, or pick up any of the dirty clothes. The fact is they have simply not grown enough to make "mature" decisions and perform certain duties. Another obvious characteristic of a baby is that he or she is taken up with personalities. As far as we know, a baby cannot look beyond a personality to have a spirit of discernment. The biggest mass murderer in America could come into their room and utter a few ga-ga's and goo-goo's and have a baby smiling. One of the most evident characteristics of a baby is that he can play while big things are happening. Some families can be going through the heartache of divorce or death, while all the time the baby is down on the floor playing with a ball. Finally, babies get easily upset. If you do not believe it, just do not give a baby a bottle at the time he thinks he needs it and see his reaction!

All of the above are signs of babes in Christ. They may be seventy years old, but if they have never matured in their faith, their feelings are the same spiritually as those babies are physically. Babies in the church always want their own way. They have no spirit of submission. They are not interested in what other church members think. Babies in the church are basically lazy. You will not find them out on outreach night or involved in other ministries.

Like physical babies, they do not give of themselves in the realm of time, talent, or tithe. Also, they are unconcerned about others. They are taken up with personalities. They have no spirit of discernment between the spirit of good and the spirit of wrong. One of the most tragic facts about babies in the church is that, like physical babies, they play when big things are happening. Tremendous transformations take place in people's lives, and people are saved and pass from darkness into light, but it really makes no difference to a spiritual baby since his greatest concern is getting to the cafeteria line and making sure the service does not go past noon. Spiritual babies also become upset easily.

We know what children need. All they need is to grow up! And it is impossible to grow up as a Christian apart from the Word of God. The early church preserved their new converts and the way they did it was through baptism, the Bible, and body life.

Baptism

The first important element in preservation is believer's baptism. In Acts 2:38-41, Peter called upon his hearers to "repent and be baptized." Why? Because it is essential in preservation. When these early believers were saved, they were immediately baptized. This is throughout the Book of Acts.

Today, we often hear some people talk about the fact that a new convert has to "prove" himself before being baptized, but this was certainly not the case in the early church.

Acts 8 recorded the baptism of the Ethiopian eunuch:

> *Then Philip began with that very passage of*
> *Scripture and told him the good news about Jesus.*
> *As they traveled along the road, they came to*
> *some water and the eunuch said, "Look, here is*
> *water. Why shouldn't I be baptized?" And he*
> *ordered the chariot to stop. Then both Philip and*
> *the eunuch went down into the water and Philip*
> *baptized him (vv. 35-38).*

In Acts 10, there was baptism in the family of Cornelius:

"Can anyone keep these people from being baptized with water? They have received the Holy Spirit just as we have"(v. 47).

In Acts 16, Lydia was baptized after her conversion:

> *One of those listening was a woman named Lydia,*
> *a dealer in purple cloth from the city of Thyatira,*
> *who was a worshiper of God. The Lord opened*
> *her heart to respond to Paul's message. When she*
> *and the members of her household were baptized,*
> *she invited us to her home. "If you consider me a*
> *believer in the Lord," she said, "come and stay at*
> *my house." And she persuaded us (vv. 14-15).*

In the same chapter the Philippian jailer was gloriously saved and immediately baptized:

> *He then brought them out and asked, "Men, what*
> *must I do to be saved?"*
> *They replied, "Believe in the Lord Jesus, and you*
> *will be saved—you and your household." Then*
> *they spoke the word of the Lord to him and to all*
> *the others in his house. At that hour of the night*
> *the jailer took them and washed their wounds;*
> *then immediately he and his family were baptized*
> *(Acts 16:30-33).*

What is baptism? It is a picture of death to the old life and resurrection to walk in newness of life (see Rom. 6:4). The truth of Scripture is you should be baptized as a confession of your faith as soon as possible after conversion. First there is *conviction* (Acts 2:37). Then there is *conversion* and *confession* (Acts 2:38). Baptism is confession for the believer. The reason many churches do not have preservation in their membership, even though they may have participation and proclamation, is because of a lack of emphasis on the first step of obedience, which is baptism.

Why do Baptists emphasize baptism so much? It is not because the water will wash away a single sin, but it is vitally important to spiritual growth and preservation. If we are not obedient to the first step of Christian growth, how are we ever going to grow? If we do not live up to the light God gives us, how are we going to expect any more light? It is no wonder that more Christians do not grow in the grace and knowledge of our Lord. So many say, "Well, I'm going to think about baptism for a while." Baptism is an essential step in preservation and Christian growth.

What is true New Testament baptism? It is best illustrated with the wedding ring. While wearing a wedding ring does not make one married, it certainly is an indication that one has made that commitment. On July 24, 1970, my wife gave me a wedding ring as we stood publicly at a wedding altar and committed our lives to each other. I have worn that ring every day since then as a means of identification regarding that commitment. She could have given me my wedding ring three months before we were married, and I could have worn it, but it would have meant nothing. Many people have been baptized before they made their commitment to Christ. Believer's baptism follows our public profession of faith.

What then, is the mode of New Testament baptism? The Greek word found here in the text is *baptizo*. It means to plunge, dip, submerge, or put under. It is used in the text no fewer than seventy-four times in the New Testament. This particular word which means to put under is not only found in the New Testament, it is extensively used in Greek literature. In Greek literature the word *baptizo* meant, in some cases, to suffer shipwreck, to sink, or to perish in the water. The story is told of a Greek sea captain whose vessel was going down and he broadcast this "mayday" message, "Baptizo, Baptizo!" (I'm sinking, I'm sinking!) Since our Lord has commanded us to be baptized, it is certainly imperative that we should desire the proper New Testament mode. This mode of baptism is immersion.

The word in the original language, found in Acts 2:41, means to immerse. It is as plain as the nose on your face when you read the Scripture. We read that baptism required "much water." Take for example John 3:23, "Now John also was baptizing at Aenon near Salim, because there was plenty of water, and people were constantly coming to be baptized." Baptism is described as a "going down into the water." "And he ordered the chariot to stop. Then both Philip and the eunuch went down into the water and Philip baptized him" (Acts 8:38).

New Testament baptism is like a "burial" under the water.

> We were therefore buried with him through
> baptism into death in order that, just as Christ
> was raised from the dead through the glory of the
> Father, we too may live a new life (Rom. 6:4).
> Now if we died with Christ, we believe that we
> will also live with him (Rom. 6:8).

New Testament baptism is described as coming up out of the water. "As soon as Jesus was baptized, he went up out of the water. At that moment heaven was opened, and he saw the Spirit of God descending like a dove and lighting on him" (Matt. 3:16). *The crystal-clear truth of Scripture is that baptism is by immersion.* And it should always follow salvation! If you have not been immersed since your salvation experience you have not undergone New Testament baptism. This is not the view of any particular church. It is the truth of Scripture. Baptism should take place after salvation and not before. Note the order in Acts 2:38, "Repent and be baptized." The same order is found in Acts 2:41: "Those who accepted his message were baptized."

There are churches which practice infant baptism. Some churches baptize babies and very young children who have not yet had a genuine salvation experience. Many of these churches use Acts 2:39 as a proof text which goes: "The promise is for you and your children and for all who are far off—for all whom the Lord our God will call." They claim infants should be baptized. But what does Acts 2:39 really teach? Read it carefully. Some take this verse and put a period after the word "children" so that it reads, "The promise is for you and your children." Thus, they insist infants ought to be sprinkled; they arguement the blessings of the covenant are for them and their children. But you cannot chop off a verse halfway and make it fit your own personal philosophy of theology.

What is Acts 2:39 actually conveying? Look at it carefully. "The promise is for you and your children *and* for all those who are far off for all whom the Lord our God will call" (author's italics). It is not only for you and your children, it is for those who are "far off." So then I may argue, "The promise is for you and your children," therefore your children should be baptized. If we go on with the text, "and for all those who are far off," then all who are far off should also be baptized. Therefore, we would be saying, all who are far off should be baptized whether they are saved or not. So goes this reasoning, and it is completely unbiblical!

What does this text actually mean? It is pointing out that this covenant promise, ". . . whosoever shall call on the name of the Lord shall be saved" (Acts 2:21, KJV), is meant for you and your children... and for those who are far off-the African natives, the negritos of New Guinea, the ebony-faced women of Ghana, the Eskimos in their igloos in Alaska, and anybody anywhere "to whom the Lord our God will call" is addressed. Someone quickly replies, "but whole households were baptized in the Book of Acts." Yes, but there is no scriptural reason to believe that in any case they did not first repent as Peter had preached in Acts 2:38. And after they had done this, then they were baptized!

Imagine the effect on Jerusalem when three thousand people came out of the shadows to identify with the Lord Jesus Christ through believer's baptism. It is no wonder the whole city was stirred and moved. It is no wonder spiritual awakening came to Jerusalem. The first step in preserving new converts is to see them through the waters of baptism. Peter unapologetically and personally appealed to his hearers to be baptized. Every church should exhort their converts to be baptized, not because the water would save them or wash away their sins, but because it is the first step in preservation, growing in the grace and knowledge of our Lord. The truth is if we do not live up to the light God has given us, we can never expect to receive any more light.

Baptism is a means of identification. There is a prevalent trend in our culture. People today like to identify with certain things or persons. Some people carry key rings with Mercedes Benz emblems, while others wear Gucci shoes with its emblem. Still others would not think of carrying anything but a Mont Blanc pen, while others would not wear a tie that was not a Hermes. People like to identify with their schools so they wear a class ring or class sweater. There are some who would not wear a sweater that did not have the emblem of Ralph Lauren. There are still others who are quick to identify with Rolex watches.

Baptism gives us an opportunity to do what we like to do. That is, identify with something. Or, rather in this case, someone! Baptism is a means of identification. It lets the world know we have identified with Jesus Christ. What makes a church great in the eyes of God? *Participation, proclamation,* and *preservation.* The first step in preservation is *baptism.*

Bible

The second step in preservation is the Bible. "They devoted themselves to the apostles' teaching" (Acts 2:42). That is, they continued in the Word of God. The word *didache* means doctrine, or translated in the *New International Version* as teaching.

This consisted of the fundamentals of the faith. They devoted themselves to such great doctrinal truths as the virgin birth of Christ, His sinless life and vicarious death, His bodily resurrection, and His second coming. They grounded themselves and continued in the great doctrinal truths of the Word of God.

We are not called merely to make decisions; we are called to make disciples. When a person is genuinely saved, one continues in the apostles' teaching. Our Lord Himself observed, "By their fruits you shall know them." There can be no preservation in the church where the Bible, and its doctrine and teaching, are not expounded and explained to the people. Many wonder why membership dwindles in some churches. It is because God blesses His Word, and when it is not used, there is no preservation. The church exploded in Jerusalem because they "devoted themselves" and continued steadfastly "in the apostles' teaching." They were rooted and grounded in the Word of God. Our only hope for preservation is the Word of God. You cannot grow in faith without that Word. You may be saved and be baptized, but if you do not devote yourself to the apostles' teaching, you will never grow in the grace and knowledge of Jesus Christ. Paul wrote to Timothy that the Word of God was "profitable." This is throughout the Scriptures. In Romans, the Bible is profitable for *doctrine*. In the Corinthian letters, the Bible is profitable for *reproof.* In Galatians, the Bible is profitable for *correction.* In Ephesians, it is profitable for *instruction in righteousness.* The Bible is like God's road map. *First, there is doctrine.* We begin down the road with Christ, and we face the amazing doctrinal truth of the Deity of Christ. He is God. When we obey and come to Christ, we are walking on the road with Him. But what happens when we veer along the road? *We see secondly that the Bible is profitable for reproof.* It reproves us and helps us recognize a wrong turn. God said, "Is not my word like . . . a hammer that breaks a rock in pieces?" (Jer. 23:29). How does one straighten out one's path? *Here we find the Bible is profitable for correction.* The word shows us how to get back on track with God, but it does not leave us there. *Finally it is profitable for instruction in righteousness* (2 Tim. 3:16-17). The Word shows us how to stay on the road so we will not wander off again. It is profitable and essential in our preservation and growth.

What makes a church great? Participation, proclamation, and preservation, which entails making much of baptism and much of the Bible.

Body Life

The third important element in preservation is body life. This body life concept is found in Acts 2:42-46:

> *They devoted themselves to the apostles' teaching and to the fellowship, to the breaking of bread and to prayer. Everyone was filled with awe, and many wonders and miraculous signs were done by the apostles. All the believers were together and had everything in common. Selling their possessions and goods, they gave to anyone as he had need. Every day they continued to meet together in the temple courts. They broke bread in their homes and ate together with glad and sincere hearts.*

These people spent their time learning, loving, and listening to each other. Great churches are characterized by this body life concept. Every member is a minister and everyone functions within the body together. There was fellowship in this early church. "They devoted themselves to the apostles' teaching and to the *fellowship*" (Acts 2:42, author's italics). The word is *koinonia*. It means they were 'all together'; and they loved each other. It was one for all and all for one. It was a shared life.

The origin of the word *koinos* (from which *koinonia* is derived) means common, not in the sense we often think of today. It meant that which people share or have together.

Consider the phrase, and they had all things common in relation to the Jerusalem church. Even in our current generation we often use the phrase, "We or they have such and such in common." It infers a like trait or characteristic.

All of us are familiar with metal money that is called a coin or coins. Those terms are straight from the Greek language. What is a coin used for? It is used for exchange, and it passes from hand to hand. Those who have phobias about germs probably think about a quarter, half dollar, or even pennies as possibly being soiled, because they have passed from hand to hand. A coin is a common piece shared by perhaps hundreds, maybe even thousands of hands.

Thus, it is with the *koinonia* we have in Christ. *Koinonia* ideally means, not merely fellowship, but a life which is shared. Every born-again, blood-bought believer has a common Savior, faith, experience, goal, and destiny. Wherever you meet another genuine Christian, you have an immediate spiritual tie. If only we could remember this, churches would have virtually no real problems because all Christians are together through "the scarlet thread" of the blood of Jesus Christ which has drawn us and sewn us together into God's tapestry of the redeemed.

Koinonia is not merely coming together to have a meal or to participate in church activities. What a word ... "what a fellowship, what a joy divine, leaning on the everlasting arms."

When a person is born again into God's family, he immediately has a kinship to every believer here and in the hereafter!

What happened? The coming and filling of the Holy Spirit caused them to live life on a higher plane of love for God and for one another. There are different Greek words which are translated into our English Bible with the word *love.* There is the word *agape* that means giving, forgiving, unreserved, or self—God's love. There is also *philos* which means tender affection, the brotherly sort of love. Prior to Pentecost, the best the apostles could do was to love on the level of *philos.* In fact, that is the best anyone can do without the Holy Spirit in his or her heart.

For example, you remember the conversation of our Lord Jesus with Simon Peter on the shore before Pentecost. John 21:15 records it. The Lord asked him, "Simon, son of John, do you love me more than these?" The word He used was *agape.*

Simon answered. "Yes, Lord, you know that I love you." Peter replied with the word *phileo.* It was the best Peter could do.

Then on the night before the crucifixion, Jesus instructed His apostles,

"A new command I give you: Love one another.
As I have loved you, so you must love one another.
All men will know that you are my disciples if you
love one another" (John 13:34-35).

Here is the word *agape.* Jesus was leaving His followers. They had watched His life for three years and up until then, the best they could do was to love on the level of *philos* love. It was the level of the old commandment which taught to "love your neighbor as yourself" (Leviticus. 19:18). But now, love was not an option. It was to be a new commandment. It was to be *agape* and not philos. The point is this: Before Pentecost one could not love properly with God's love, because it is impossible without the Spirit's love burning within us. This love came into the disciples when they were filled with the Holy Spirit, and thus they "continued steadfastly, devoting themselves to fellowship." This is why Paul later wrote in Galatians 5:22, "the fruit of the Spirit is love" *(agape)*.

This has so many applications. For example, this is why it is essential for a Christian to marry another believer and not an unbeliever. Try as he may, an unbeliever can never love a mate with the highest level of love, the most selfless kind of love *(agape),* because it is only found in Jesus Christ.

We need each other. Great churches are made up of great fellowship. We can be baptized and be in the Bible but still cannot grow without this concept of body life *fellowship.* We need each other. There has never been a great church in the eyes of God without this element of fellowship. Some "professed believers" have such little fellowship with the people of God. We all ought to ask ourselves if we are merely singing hymns, saying words, and coming to meetings, just going through the motions. Some of us live like the world, think like the world, talk like the world, act like the world, and then go to church, watch our watches, and if the service goes over an hour we fidget. At the same time, we can go to a ball game, movie, or party and say, "How time flies," when we have been there three hours or more. And you tell me you are going to go to heaven, praise the Lord, and fellowship with the people of God there when you do not desire that fellowship here. Who are you kidding? Yourself!

What makes a great church? Participation, proclamation, and preservation. Preservation involves baptism, the Bible, and body life. The first part of body life is *fellowship,* but there is also the importance of the *"breaking of bread"* (Acts 2:42, author's italics). That is the Lord's Supper. Luke does not simply refer to having meals together. He makes the point that the early church came together to share in the symbolic testimony of the body and blood of Christ which is the basis of the Christian life. What is the breaking of bread? It is the Lord's Supper—the unleavened bread and the cup of unfermented juice from the vine. We have continued in this until this very day. It is a part of our preservation.

They also devoted themselves to "prayer" (see Acts 2:42). They continued in prayer. This is how they began. For ten days they prayed in the upper room. Some of us begin but never continue. Please note that they "devoted themselves" to prayer, not just in teaching, fellowship, and breaking of bread, but to prayer, beseeching the Lord at the throne of grace.

They also had a sharing spirit. Acts 2:42-44 says,
"They devoted themselves to the apostles' teaching and to the fellowship, to the breaking of bread and to prayer." Everyone was filled with awe, and many wonders and miraculous signs were done by the apostles. All the believers were together and had everything in common."

They had the theme that every member was a minister. I doubt if they said, "Let Peter do it," or "Let's let Joseph of Aramathea pull a string with the United Way of Jerusalem." Everyone was together, and they all did their part.

Some contend that this sounds like communism, a form of socialism. There was no communism in Acts 2. These people believed in God; this was church-controlled and not state-controlled; it was voluntary; and it was obviously temporary. Many Jews were away from home in Jerusalem for the Passover Feast. We do not read about it happening later in the early church, but the point is they had this concept of body life!

Another concept of body life was "gladness and singleness of heart" (Acts 2:46, KJV). This was a joyful church. A gloomy Christian is a contradiction in terms. Joy filled the atmosphere of the presence of these people at Pentecost.

Another aspect of their body life was worship and praise (Acts 2:46-47). Praise is the secret of the liberated life! There is power in praise. "God inhabits the praises of his people," and we are to praise Him in song, word, and action. The truth is we cannot grow in grace and knowledge of our Lord without being involved in personal praise. In Ephesians 5:18, we find the command, "be filled with the Spirit," and in the next verse we notice the result in "singing and making melody in our hearts to the Lord" (Eph. 5:19, KJV).

What makes a church great in the eyes of God? *Participation* and *proclamation* but also *preservation.* How is this preservation obtained? Through *baptism,* the *Bible,* and *body-life* concept.

Chapter Ten

Propagation

Praising God and enjoying the favor of all the people. And the Lord added to their number daily those who were being saved (Acts 2:47).

A church can have participation, proclamation, and preservation, but if the church does not have the element of propagation, it will never be a great church in the eyes of God. This early church went everywhere witnessing. The propagation of the gospel fulfilled Acts 1:8 in one day. And the result was the "Lord added to their number daily those who were being saved." They propagated the gospel in a winsome way and a winning way.

If we are ever to see the church truly revived again in our generation, then we must lay hold of this concept of equipping the saints to do the work of the ministry. This first-century church went everywhere sharing their faith and performing the works of ministry.

The churches in our day and age who are seeing mercy drops of revival are those who have mobilized their people to do the work of ministry. These are churches which have all kinds of ministries but only one overriding purpose, and that is to glorify and honor the Lord Jesus by fulfilling the Great Commission to make, mark, and mature believers in the faith.

Example

To begin with, mobilization is done by example. If

pastors are going to mobilize their people as we move the church into the twenty-first century, then we must be on the cutting edge ourselves, and our people must see that we do not ask them to do something we do not do ourselves. The best way to mobilize people for the work of ministry is by *example*. Perhaps Gideon expressed it best when, as he led his small army to face the Midianites, he said, "Do as I do!" These pointed words may be the epitaph of many churches today. That is, they do what the pastor does. My pastor used to tell all of his preacher boys: "Never use your people to build your ministry, but always use your ministry to build your people."

Expectancy

Another important element in the mobilization of people to the work of the ministry is expectancy. Here is the spirit of conquest. A vision, if you please. Someone has commented that a "vision without a task is simply a dream. A task without a vision is drudgery. But a vision with a task is the hope of the world."

Environment

Another key element in the mobilization of people to propagate the gospel is found in the word *environment*. In my opinion the two greatest factors in church growth are love and unity among the fellowship. This hurting, wounded world is looking for true love and true unity.

On the evening before the crucifixion, Jesus said, "A new commandment I give unto you, That ye love one another; as *I have loved you*" (John 13:34, KJV, author's italics). For thirty-three years Jesus had given us a picture of what real love truly is. Until then, the best we could do was live on the level of the old commandment found in Leviticus 19:18, "Love your neighbor as yourself." But some of us have a real problem there. That is, we have no self-worth or self-respect, and if we loved others as we love ourselves, we would not be loving with very deep love. But after thirty-three years of demonstrating what true love really is, Jesus said, "Love one another as I have loved you." The environment of love is the most important ingredient in church growth, and it is also the most basic factor in mobilizing people to propagate the gospel.

Not only is love important to the environment but also to unity. I believe the pastor's primary job is to "maintain the unity of the spirit and the bond of peace." Personally, unity is what I guard more than all else in our church. The most important factor in a family is unity. The most important factor in an athletic team is unity. The most important factor in a business is unity. And a church should be known by its unity. I am not speaking about uniformity but unity. There is a tremendous difference. Uniformity is an outward expression while unity is an inward expression. There is diversity in unity. We are not all alike, but we can all be together.

Exertion

Another important word in mobilizing people to the propagation of the gospel is exertion. We are to equip the saints to do "the work of the ministry." And the ministry is work! When we are truly walking in the Spirit, we will not be wearing out the seats of our pants but the soles of our shoes. So often I hear that this church or that church simply operates "in the flesh." Well, the fact is, that is what our Spirit-filled lives have to operate within.

As we follow the life of Jesus, we discover that He

exerted Himself so many times in so many ways. He had a special affinity toward the outcast. Jesus loves the rejects and pariahs of society. When He went to Jerusalem, where did He go? To the pool of Bethesda where handicapped persons were lying near the pool. When He went through Jericho where did He go? Did He make a beeline to meet the mayor to receive the key to the city? No, He went to a blind beggar rattling a cup on the side of the road. When He passed through Samaria did He have an "I-know-the-governor syndrome" like so many of us preachers today? No, He didn't go to the governor. He was interested in a sinful woman outside the city at Jacob's Well. He met her in the middle of the day to give her living water. Some of us need to stop being so hypocritical as we sit pompously behind our stained-glass walls talking about how much we care about missions in darkest Africa when we are uncomfortable having a Haitian refugee sitting beside us on the pew. Revival comes when folks do not mind getting their hands dirty in something that is real.

Encouragement

We also find that another element of mobilizing people to the propagation of the gospel is encouragement. Nothing mobilizes people more than encouragement, words of appreciation, exhortation, and encouragement. As we read the Book of Acts, we find those early believers continually encouraging one another in the faith. If the church is going to be revived again in our day, it is not enough simply to have the element of participation or proclamation or preservation. We must become caught up in propagation and burst outside the four walls of our buildings, mobilizing our people to do the work of the ministry and carrying the gospel to the four corners of the world!

Note that they propagated the gospel in a winsome way.
The Bible says they were "enjoying the favor of all the
people" (Acts 2:47). The religious system of the day rejected
these early believers. They were a threat to the traditional
religion. Also, the Roman government rejected them
because they would not bow down and say, "Caesar is Lord."
But the truth is that most of the people embraced them.
They "enjoyed the favor of all the people." They were
winsome in their witness and in their worship, and thousands
were converted because of it.

Real Christianity is lovely. There is a quality about a
spirit-filled, radiant Christian that draws and attracts others
and causes them to "enjoy favor with all the people." The
truth is that the gospel is not nearly as offensive as some of
its proponents! People were attracted to these early
believers' joy and wanted to know the source of it.
Evangelism in this first-century church was more caught
than taught. This is how it should be in the twenty-first
century church.

They also propagated the gospel in a winning way. "And
the Lord added to their number daily those who were being
saved" (Acts 2:47). They were a growing church! Every
once in awhile we hear someone remark, "I like to be part
of a small, spiritual church." There is no such thing as a
small, spiritual church in a metropolitan area. I understand
that population makes a difference. If the church is spiritual,
it will be healthy, and if it is healthy, it will be growing! If
you are the type of person who does not want to be part of
a large church, you certainly would not have wanted to be a
member of the first church in Jerusalem in the first-century.

What do I mean? Let's see! In Acts 1:15, there were
120 believers. Someone says, "Oh, we like it like that."
There are many churches like that. They are often governed

by people who want something they can control. Often they cannot control anything at work or at home, so they might join a little church and develop a "God complex." They want to be served; they do not want to serve. They want a preacher to stroke them and pat them on the back. All the while the whole world is going to hell, and they want a church they can control. This early church was a healthy church, and because it was healthy it was filled with participation, proclamation, preservation, and it propagated the gospel so it grew in grace and numbers. Some 3,000 were added. Then 5,000 more. Then, we are told it "multiplied."

Here we see these early believers being faithful to our Lord's last words to them, "But you will receive power when the Holy Spirit comes on you; and you will be my witnesses in Jerusalem, and in all Judea and Samaria, and to the ends of the earth" (Acts 1:8).

They had come to grips with five important questions which had arisen out of these last words of our Lord. Now, having been endued with power from on high, they were fulfilling Acts 1:8 in their generation.

First, they dealt with the question of *who*. Here is an imperative in the future tense. No one was excluded. The point is, none of us are beyond this commission of Christ to be witnesses of His saving grace.

Next we deal with the question of *what*. They were to receive what? Power! Here is the urgent need of the church today. Many churches are anemic in their worship and in their witness. The word translated *power (dunamis)* is the same word from which we receive our word *dynamite*. It may be that the difference in the first-century church and the twenty-first century church is in two words—influence and power. While the church of our day prides itself in influence (particularly in the political realm), it has so little power. The early church did not have enough influence to keep Peter out of prison but had enough power to pray him out!

Next, they dealt with the question of *when.* When? When would this power come upon them? "When the Holy Spirit comes upon you." The Holy Spirit within is Who gives power. We need to strengthen our witness that comes from a source that is outside of us. We need the dynamic power of the Holy Spirit within us, and when we are being filled with the Holy Spirit, witnessing will become as natural as water running downhill. Like Peter and the other apostles, we cannot "help but speak the things we have seen and heard."

They also dealt with the question of *why.* Why were they to receive power when the Holy Spirit came upon them? There is only one reason: "To be my witnesses." If you are saved, you have Christ, and He has you. If you have Christ, you have the Holy Spirit. If you have the Holy Spirit, you have power. If you have power, you are a witness. Note that He does not fill us with the Holy Spirit in order for us to become the judge, prosecuting attorney, defense, or jury but the witness.

We are witnesses unto Christ. We are not recruiters trying to induce people to join our club. We are not sales representatives trying to sell people our products. We are witnesses of Jesus Christ and His saving grace. The mark of a carnal church is that it talks about itself and invites people to come hear its preacher, or to attend its Sunday School. The mark of a mature church is that it talks about the Lord Jesus Christ and is a witness unto Him.

This early church also dealt with the question of *where.* Where is this gospel to be taken as we are filled with God's

Holy Spirit? The gospel is to be taken across the city, across the country, across the continent, and across the cosmos. There is a sense in which Acts 1:8 is an outline for the rest of the book. They took the gospel to Jerusalem in Acts 1-8. They took the gospel through Judea and Samaria in Acts 9-12. They took the gospel to the ends of the earth in Acts 13-28. In thirty years this exciting early church fulfilled Acts 1:8. There is an important point for the church of our day. We cannot play leapfrog with the Great Commission. Witnessing for Christ begins in our own Jerusalem, not the ends of the earth. The highest form of hypocrisy is for mission groups to talk about how much they want to win people to Christ on foreign fields when they will not even share Jesus Christ with their next-door neighbor. Propagating the gospel begins at home and continues until it reaches the end of the world!

Many lament that taking the gospel to the whole world is a mammoth task for the twenty-first century church. What a task it must have been for the first-century church.

It looked *geographically* impossible. Many believed the world was still flat! It appeared to be *physically* impossible. There was no air travel, no printing press, no radio, no television, no telephone, no facsimile machine and no Internet. It looked *legally* impossible. It was against the law to speak in Christ's name in many places. It looked *socially* impossible. The church was made up of so many rejects and outcasts of society.

How did they do it? They received power when the Holy Spirit came upon them and then they propagated the gospel to the ends of the world. They went where people are in need of the gospel of Jesus Christ.

The church must do this if it is ever going to be revived again. We need to remember Jesus did not die in a starched white shirt and tie on a gold cross on some white communion table within the stained-glass walls of some high-steeple church. He died where thieves were cursing and soldiers were gambling, and that is where we are to go, "To the ends of the earth." We are to penetrate the whole world until "the darkness shall turn to dawning. And the dawning to noonday bright. And Christ's great kingdom shall come on earth, the kingdom of love and light" (H. Ernest Nichol).

By Acts 2:41, we read "three thousand were added to their number that day." Now there were 3,000 and 120. In Acts 2:47, it says, "the Lord added to their number daily"; In Acts 4:4, "The number of men grew to about five thousand." The word for men used in Acts 4:4 is *andros.* It is a word used for man in the masculine sense as opposed to a woman. These were five thousand *men,* and it is likely their families were also saved. Some believe as many as fifteen to twenty thousand were saved by the time of this account in Acts 4:4. It is very possible then that the church numbered around 25,000 members. In Acts 5:28, we read that the message of Christ had "filled Jerusalem." Oh, what a day!

If only in our cities of America today, we might one day hear that our cities were filled with the good news of Jesus. In Acts 6:7, the number of disciples "increased rapidly." King James translators rendered this verse to read "multiplied greatly." Now, we are no longer talking about addition but multiplication. How many were in the early church? While no one knows for sure, Dr. B. H. Carroll, the founder of Southwestern Baptist Theological Seminary, thought there were 65,000 members the first six months. G. Campbell Morgan, the late, great pastor of Westminster Chapel in London, figures there were 250,000 converted in the first six months of the church in Jerusalem. The point is they propagated the gospel in a winsome way and in a winning way.

What makes a church great in the eyes of God? Participation, proclamation, preservation, and propagation. We must have all four! There are some churches who have participation. They live together in unity and make much of the filling of the Holy Spirit but have no preservation. There are others who have proclamation and make much of the Bible but who have no participation, no sense of belonging to God, much less to one another. There are still others who make much of propagation but who have no sense of preservation of new converts. Great churches in the eyes of God, like the Jerusalem church, are characterized by a balanced ministry that involves all four elements. This is what the church needs today. Oh, that the church of Jesus Christ today would live together in unity, be filled with the Holy Spirit, make much of the Word of God in proclamation, preserve their new converts to grow in grace and knowledge, and go outside the four walls of their church to propagate the Gospel in a winsome and winning way. If this would only happen, our land would be filled with the message of Jesus Christ.

One of the blessings of my own personal devotional life is to pray the great hymns of the faith. As I concluded these writings of the early church I found myself praying through my spirit the words of that great old hymn:

Lord, as of old at Pentecost, Thou didst Thy power display
With cleansing purifying flame, Descend on us today.
For mighty works for Thee, Prepare and strengthen every heart
Come, take possessions of Thine own, And never

more depart.

All self consume, all sin destroy, With earnest zeal endue

Each waiting heart to work for Thee, O Lord, our faith renew.

Speak, Lord! Before Thy throne we wait

Thy promise we believe

And will not let thee go until Thy blessing we receive.

Lord, send the old time power, The Pentecostal power

Thy flood gates of blessing, On us open wide.

Lord, send the old time power, The Pentecostal power

That sinners be converted, And thy name be glorified

Lyrics by CHARLES H. GABRIEL

May God's special blessings rest upon that church that manifests its ministry with "SHIELDS OF GOLD" in participation, proclamation, preservation, and propagation. And may our continual prayer be that we will not substitute shields of brass for shields of gold.

Part Four

The No Fear Culture

NO FEAR...those two words seem to be tattooed across our culture. In fact, they even form the brand name of a popular apparel company. No Fear Jeans speaks volumes about who we have become in our current culture.

Unfortunately, in a day when the culture of a secular society has infiltrated the church it has brought with it a "no fear" philosophy. When was the last time you heard a message in the modern church cover a topic like the fear of the Lord? When was the last time you even heard anyone mention such a thing as the fear of the Lord? And yet, this phrase, "the fear of the Lord", finds itself woven throughout the fabric of over three hundred verses in the Bible.

Our western culture is in the midst of a serious credibility and integrity crisis. Our insistence on moral leadership has descended to such a level that Presidential moral scandals are more commonplace than out of the ordinary. This climate really says more about the American people than it does the American President. It says more about the American pew than it does the American people. The salt has lost it's savor. But, in reality, it says even more about the American pulpit than it does the American pew.

What is missing in the church today? The difference in the modern church and the early church is found in two words—influence and power. As noted previously, the early church did not have enough influence to keep Simon Peter out of jail but they had enough power to pray him out. Today the church speaks little of any kind of spiritual power while it prides itself on it's influence. The early church engaged it's culture and transformed it. What did they have that we seem to have lost? In so many ways we have so much more than they did. We are far more educated. We have far more in the way of technological advances to be used in kingdom expansion. We have television, radio, air travel, e-mail, computers, the Internet and our personal web pages. But along the way we have lost something very important. We have lost the concept of "walking in the fear of the Lord." It is said of the early church that they "had peace and were edified and walking in the fear of the Lord and in the comfort of the Holy Spirit they were multiplied")" (Acts 9:31).

What an incredible insight—they were "walking in the fear of the Lord." Who is doing that today? Who even knows what it means much less gives it a thought? So much of the church in the western world today is anemic in confronting the culture. Many modern church growth gurus encourage us to minister by polling data and popular opinion. We often criticize those in politics for abdicating true leadership in favor of leading by the popular polling data they have obtained and then simply furnishing their constituents with what they want instead of what they need. But the church so often does the same thing. One church recently revealed how their musical selections for worship were selected by doing a survey of what radio stations their congregants enjoyed. Music style was then determined by the wants of the people. Such completely man-centered ministries ultimately dethrone doctrinal truths related to the nature of God, the nature of man, and the nature of sin in favor of a self help, feel-good-about-yourself philosophy that is void of the idea of "walking in the fear of the Lord."

Many churches today are filled with "felt need" hearers and "how to" motivational messages. Some even refer to it as a New Reformation centered on the importance of self esteem which has little mention of such things as sin, judgment or the fear of the Lord and consequently, less mention of the need of anything as drastic and archaic as repentance. In many circles the pastor is looked upon more in terms of a corporate executive whose main concern lies in the realm of marketing and sales.

We have raised a couple of generations in America who do not know the "rest of the story." We are convinced that people prefer to hear about God's love, mercy, kindness and his unconditional acceptance regardless of our lifestyles. When the subject of God's wrath, judgement, or fear surfaces many are quick to respond, "Oh, my God is not like that." The monthly periodical "Current Thoughts and Trends" in it's April 1998 edition gives the following quote from Robert Schuller—"I don't think anything has been done in the name of Christ and under the banner of Christianity that has proven more destructive to human personality, and hence counterproductive to the evangelistic enterprise, than the unchristian, uncouth strategy of attempting to make people aware of their lost and sinful condition." (quoted in *Milk & Honey*, December 1997, page 4).

In the midst of a modern "no fear" culture many churches are emerging into what appears to be nothing more than impressive self help clubs and motivational assemblies. Much of what takes place in modern church growth philosophy today is foreign to a New Testament pattern of church growth. "Walking in the fear of the Lord" is one of the lost elements in modern church growth mentality and methodology. Why is "the fear of the Lord" the lost phrase in our church vocabulary? What is the "fear of the Lord?" How can it be rediscovered in our generation? Why? What? How? Let's read on.

Chapter Eleven

A Why Question

Why is it that we live with a "no fear" mentality in our culture? Perhaps it is because our generation knows little of the nature of God. We have lost a sense of the holiness of God. This reverence has been exchanged for a "good buddy" image of God. Shields of brass for shields of gold. Some of us are out of balance in our market-driven approach to church health and growth. We often tailor our church ministries to appeal to the selfish, self-centered desires of those we are striving to reach.

There is little mention of the nature of a holy God in the modern church. We have replaced him with the idea of a sort of contemporary "buddy" who is into back slapping and giving high fives. Job did not see God on this level. When confronted with the holiness of God he said, "I abhor myself and repent in sackcloth and ashes." When Isaiah caught a glimpse of the glory of God he said, "Woe is me for I am undone." When John saw God's holiness and glory on Patmos, the Bible says he "fell down at his feet as a dead man." We have developed an ecclesiastical "no fear" of God culture primarily because, in a dearth of doctrinal truth, we have lost our concept of the holiness and awesomeness of our Creator God.

We have so lost our way and have such little discernment that we compliment the Hollywood elite for such television offerings as "Touched by an Angel." Christians clamor about how wonderful it is to have a prime time television program so enthralled with angels. Hi-tech preachers show film clips of it to illustrate their messages (we do not call them sermons anymore). Tess, the angel played by Della Reese in this television series, is a far cry from angels we read about in the Bible. She is a mixture of new age deceptions. This angel tells us "there is a piece of God in each of you." She sounds more like what might emerge out of the philosophy of the church that Reese helped found called "Understanding Principles of Better Living" than the angels of scripture. This angel who denies the necessity of the cross and promotes a feel good, no condemnation approach to human problems, is embraced by a world that is searching for spiritual truth. Should we be surprised that the Bible warns of those who masquerade as "angels of light" twisting the word, hiding the gospel, and offering false promises that tend to blind the eyes of unbelievers and believers alike?

The Lord Jesus came to bring forgiveness to sinners, not to tell them that they are all right and that they simply have a self-esteem problem. He said the world hated him because he testified that it's works were evil (John 7:7). While more and more churches place doctrinal truth on the bottom shelf in favor of a self-help, market-driven approach, the church knows less and less of a holy God and never even thinks of "walking in the fear of the Lord."

This concept of the fear of the Lord held a prominent place in Old Testament Jewish worship. We remember how Noah "moved with Godly fear built the ark" (Hebrews 11:7). Before dying on Mt. Nebo, Moses challenged the Israelites with a question, "Now Israel, what does the Lord your God require of you, but to fear the Lord your God..."(Deuteronomy 10:12 NKJV). Then years later after the conquest of the promised land, his successor, Joshua, assembled the people and said, "Now, fear the Lord and serve him with all faithfulness" (Joshua 24:14). This element of "walking in the fear of the Lord" winds its way throughout the experiences of the Old Testament saints. This same emphasis found it's way into the gospels during the ministry of Christ. The virgin Mary herself, with the Christ alive in her womb, reminds us of this in her sweet song as she sings, "His mercy is on those who fear him"(Luke 1:50). When Zacharias' speech returned after the birth of John the Baptist it is said that "fear came upon all them that dwelt around them" (Luke 1:65). This attitude of fear, a holy reverence, is prevalent among believers all through the gospels. After the Lord healed the paralytic man, the Bible records that those who observed this miracle "were all amazed and they glorified God and were filled with fear" (Luke 5:26 NKJV). Again, when Jesus visited the city of Nain and healed the widow's son, the Bible records that "fear came upon them all, and they glorified God saying, "A great prophet has risen up among us and God has visited his people"(Luke 7:16 NKJV). When the Lord Jesus sent out the twelve he said, "Do not fear those who kill the body but who cannot kill the soul. But rather fear Him who is able to destroy both soul and body in hell." (Matthew 10:28 NKJV). And after the resurrection it is said of the women who came to the empty tomb that they "departed quickly from the tomb with fear and great joy, and ran to bring his disciples word" (Matthew 28:8 NKJV).

Not only do we find the concept of "walking in the fear of the Lord" woven through the Old Testament and the gospels, it also appears on practically every page in the Book of Acts describing the early church. It was there at the birth of the church. After Peter's remarkable Pentecostal proclamation "fear came upon every soul and many wonders and signs were done through the apostles" (Acts 2:43

NKJV). In Acts five, when Ananias and Sapphira met their untimely death at the hands of the Holy Spirit, the Bible records that "great fear came upon all the church" (Acts 5:11 NKJV). After the conversion of Saul of Tarsus we read that the early church ceased growing by addition and began to multiply and went forward "walking in the fear of the Lord" (Acts 9:31 NKJV). When Simon Peter preached to Cornelius' household in Caesarea by the Sea he proclaimed that "in every nation whoever fears God and works righteousness is accepted by Him" (Acts 10:35 NKJV). In the great Apostle Paul's first recorded sermon at Pisidian Antioch, he addressed his hearers with these words—"Men of Israel and you who fear God listen..."(Acts 13:16 NKJV). When Paul visited Ephesus and performed miracles we are told that "fear fell on them all and the name of the Lord Jesus was magnified" (Acts 19:17 NKJV). One can not read the account of the Book of Acts without seeing the prominent part that "walking in the fear of the Lord" played in the explosive growth of the first century called-out ones.

When we close the pages of the Acts of the Apostles and move into the epistles we find this theme continuing to weave its way throughout the whole Bible. Paul spoke often of it to the first century churches and to us. To the Romans he lamented a people who had "no fear of God before their eyes" (Romans 3:18 NKJV). He admonished us in this dispensation of grace to "stand by faith, do not be haughty, but fear" (Romans 11:20 NKJV). To the Corinthians he said, "Therefore, having these promises, beloved, let us cleanse ourselves from all filthiness of the flesh and the spirit, perfecting holiness in the fear of God" (2 Corinthians 7:1 NKJV). He continues by reminding them that Titus' "affections are greater for you as he remembers the obedience of you all, how with fear and trembling you received him" (2 Corinthians 7:15 NKJV). In an often quoted passage to those at Ephesus he reminds us to "submit to one another in the fear of God"(Ephesians 5:21).

Other New Testament writers beat this same drum. The writer of Hebrews sums it up by saying, "Therefore since we are receiving a kingdom which cannot be shaken, let us have grace, by which we may serve God acceptably with reverence and godly fear" (Hebrews 12:28 NKJV). Simon Peter in his epistle admonishes us to "Honor all people. Love the brotherhood. Fear God. Honor the king." (1 Peter 2:17 NKJV). In one of the most personally challenging passages in the Bible, Peter calls upon believers to "sanctify the Lord God in your hearts, and always be ready to give a defense to everyone who asks you a reason for the hope that is in you, with meekness and fear" (1 Peter 3:15 NKJV).

Not only is the idea of the importance of "walking in the fear of the Lord" woven throughout the Old Testament, and the gospels and the Acts of the Apostles, and the epistles, but it is there in the apocalypse. In that coming grand and glorious day when the amens and alleluias are heard around the throne we are told there will be a great voice coming from the throne saying, "Praise our God all you his servants and those who fear Him both small and great!" (Revelation 19:5 NKJV).

The modern church is faced with a why question. Why do we have a "no fear" culture in the modern church? The Old Testament saints, those in the gospels, those in the early church and those gathered around the throne in heaven all have something in common that is separate and apart from much we see in the church of today. What is the missing element? Those before us were all found "walking in the fear of the Lord." Our church culture has little concept of the holiness and awesomeness of God. We have forgotten that God is watching, that "the eyes of the Lord are in every place keeping watch on the evil and the good" (Proverbs 15:3). Do we really believe that truth will win in the end? Our "no fear" culture scoffs at the idea of future divine judgment. It is seldom, if ever, mentioned in modern popular pulpits.

The concept of the fear of the Lord is the single most important missing element in the church of the Lord Jesus Christ in our day. The answer to the question of "why" lies in the fact that many of us have lost our sense of reverence and awe in our relationship with our Sovereign Lord. When we rediscover the holiness of God, which comes in understanding the great doctrinal truths, we will have the same healthy and wholesome fear that characterized the Old Testament saints, those who followed Christ in the gospels, and those who made up the early church. Then, we too will know the power and peace which comes with "walking in the fear of the Lord."

Chapter Twelve

A What Question

What is the "fear of the Lord?" Does it mean we must live in constant fright and flight? Does it mean that we must live in fear of God in the way one might be who is terrorized by a gang leader in the neighborhood? Is it living with the idea that God has a big hammer and is just waiting to smash us at the slightest sin we might commit? There are many who have grown up with physically or emotionally abusive parents who might confuse the idea of "the fear of the Lord" with the unhealthy fear of an abusive father or mother. Few really know what it is to be "walking in the fear of the Lord" as did those in scripture who came before us.

In the Old Testament the most common Hebrew word translated into our English word, "fear", means to stand in awe with reverence and respect. This word describes one who recognizes the power, purity, and position of another and offers him respect. This concept is hard to find in an ecclesiastical culture that prides itself on portraying God as one of the boys who is often addressed in prayer like one would address another over a hamburger. We are losing our sense of reverential awe in our relationship with the Father.

The most common word used in the New Testament to translate this word "fear" can best be described as a reverential fear of God as a controlling motive of life in matters both spiritual and moral. This is not so much a fear of his awesome power and righteous retribution as it is a wholesome fear of displeasing Him. When you read of the fear of the Lord in scripture, it is not there to make you feel like you have to cower down in His presence in fear of being hit or slapped down or embarrassed. It is the thought of bowing before Him in awe and reverence for who He really is, an awesome creator God in total control of his creation and worthy of all respect, love, praise, and worship. When we are daily "walking in the fear of the Lord" it moves us to a submissive recognition of his Lordship and results in a passionate longing to live in trust and obedience.

The fear of the Lord is a healthy concept for the believer. It is a reverential awe, a sense of being afraid of offending a holy God in any way. It is not simply intellectual assent to an idea. It is a consciousness the believer lives with continuously. It comes from a daily surrender of our lives to Christ. Surrender. Now there is a word we seldom hear today. Preachers of old used to call men and women to "surrender" their lives to Christ. We used to sing, "All to Jesus I surrender." Not today. We are too self-sufficient for such a concept. We speak of flexing our own spiritual muscles. Today we speak of "committing" our lives to Christ. "Walking in the fear of the Lord" does not come from a pumped-up kind of a self-induced commitment, but from a surrender to Jesus Christ as Lord.

What happens to a church culture when "walking in the fear of the Lord" is a forgotten concept? There emerges a sort of antinomianistic attitude that exhibits little restraint of evil. Paul speaks of a people who had "no fear of God before their eyes" (Romans 3:10-18). Moral failures by pulpit ministers are epidemic in our generation. Within a short period before this writing, several Southern Baptist pastors of my personal acquaintance have shocked their churches and devastated their families. One left his family and his church for a woman in his wife's prayer group. Another left his family and his church in favor of his former secretary. Another returned from a mission trip to announce he had fallen in love with a fellow traveler, resigned his church and walked away from his family. Another left his wife and children and pulpit to move in with a woman he had met on the internet. And still another resigned his church after being arrested for picking up a prostitute in his city. And the beat goes on! How does this happen? Could it be we are reaping the results of a generation of church leaders who have "no fear of God before their eyes?"

There are other by-products of one who does not walk in the fear of the Lord. There is little respect for submission to authority. Paul admonishes us to be "submitting to one another in the fear of God" (Ephesians 5:21). Do we wonder why there is such a problem with submission to authority in the home, at school, in the work place, in the civic arena? When the salt loses its savor, when the church ceases to engage its culture, when we have no concept of "walking in the fear of the Lord," a lack of submission is the natural result.

The church we read about in Acts saw corruption and attack from without. They came under tremendous persecution at the hands of the Roman empire. As we enter the third millennium, no longer is our danger from without as much as from within. We seem to be living in the book of Jude. Jude spoke of a church that would become corrupt from within. He metaphorically presents a shocking picture of what is taking place in much of modern church growth. He speaks of a day when churches would be led and attended by those who are "without fear" (Jude 12). He describes the individual who has "no fear of God before his eyes" as a hidden reef, a cloud without rain, a tree without fruit, a wild wave of the sea, and a wandering star out of orbit.

Jude describes several characteristics of those in the church who manage and minister "without fear." He says they *lack peace*. He uses the metaphor of "a hidden reef in your love feast." The picture is one of hidden rocks or reefs below the surface of the water and unnoticed by the naked eye. These unexpected dangers can cause a boat to be grounded and to begin to leak. Many churches sailing across the waters of love and fellowship have been "grounded" by individuals who lived "without fear" and who destroyed the unity of the fellowship of faith.

Jude also indicates that these types of people within the church also *lack productivity*. They are, in his words, like "clouds without water carried about by the wind." They appear to be full of wonderful prospects for the future. However, they are simply filled with empty promises. They never really spiritually produce. They look good and say all the right words, but they possess nothing of substance and they are simply blown around by the next thing that comes out of a success magazine.

Jude says these individuals who live "without fear" are exposed not only by a lack of peace and a lack of productivity, but a *lack of proof.* They are like "autumn trees without fruit." The Lord Jesus said, "You will know them by their fruits." (Matthew 7:16).

He continues by showing another characteristic by which these disrespectful people may be known. They also *lack purity.* In Jude's words they are like "raging waves of the sea foaming up their own shame." That is, they will eventually expose themselves. For fifteen years I lived on the Atlantic Coast. When the weather is calm, the ocean is crystal clear. But when the storms come and the winds of the hurricane season begin to blow, the ocean begins to churn. Those raging waves bring up the filth and debris from the ocean floor and deposit it with its foam upon the shore. A beach stroll in the aftermath of a storm reveals a multitude of rotting dead fish and all sorts of trash from the ocean floor now on the beach for all to see. Jude says that those who live "without fear" are eventually exposed by their lack of purity.

Finally, he illustrates one other characteristic, a *lack of purpose*. Jude says these individuals are like "wandering stars for whom is reserved the blackness of darkness forever." Those who are not "walking in the fear of the Lord" have no real direction, nor purpose, in life. Who of us has not seen a shooting star, a piece of the cosmos gone wrong, out of orbit, racing across the night sky. Its brilliance is dazzling. And then, as quickly as it appeared, it disappears into the darkness of the night. God placed the stars in courses in the heavens. Stars have orbits in which they operate. They have direction and purpose. Those "without fear" are like these wandering stars out of orbit. They do not want any structure. They do not like things like statements of faith. They do not want to play within any boundaries.

In a "no fear" culture that has invaded the church of the Lord Jesus Christ we need more than ever to "contend earnestly for the faith which was for all delivered to the saints." (Jude 3).

When the church is "walking in the fear of the Lord" the result is vibrant and productive. Recently, my home church had a reunion of hundreds of us who were active during our high school and college years. It had been a quarter of a century since some of us had seen one other. I had no real church background until I was converted at the age of seventeen. My life was radically transformed and I immersed myself in the life and ministry of the Sagamore Hill Baptist Church in Fort Worth, Texas. Our pastor and role model, Dr. W. Fred Swank, was pastor there for over forty years and over one hundred young men surrendered to the gospel ministry and are preaching around the world today as a result of God's call and our pastor's example and encouragement.

Going back "home" after all those years brought back a myriad of memories. I saw several girls I had dated as a young man, now middle-aged like myself, whom I had not seen in years. I was thankful I could look them all in the eye with no regrets. I had remained morally pure. How? We were all tempted in our day as young people are today. But we had something few young people seem to have today. We had a healthy and wholesome concept of the "fear of the Lord." It was not the fear of being beaten down by God for any little slip along the way. It was a reverence, an awe, of his presence and holiness which we acquired from hearing Him lifted up and exalted from a Bible preacher whom we loved and respected and who was himself a paragon of faithfulness. My fear was not that He might lay a hand on me but that He might take his hand off me! I feared disappointing God who had done so much for me.

When we are "walking in the fear of the Lord" there is imparted to us a power to overcome our sinful desires and habits. Solomon reminds us that "by the fear of the Lord one departs from evil" (Proverbs 16:6). After receiving the law on Sinai, Moses told his people that "God has come test you and that his fear may be before you so that you may not sin" (Exodus 20:20).

When we are "walking in the fear of the Lord" there also comes to us a supernatural wisdom and understanding. The wisest man who ever lived put it like this—"The fear of the Lord is the beginning of wisdom" (Proverbs 9:10). It also is the avenue into true worship. David said, "In fear of you I will worship toward Your holy temple" (Psalm 5:7 NKJV). "Walking in the fear of the Lord" was a constant theme of the psalmist. He relates how it can bring supernatural deliverance. "The angel of the Lord encamps all around those that fear Him and delivers them." (Psalm 34:7). It is a channel through which the mercy of the Lord can flow to you. The psalmist says, "Great is His mercy toward those that fear Him" (Psalm 103:11). When we "walk in the fear of the Lord" it brings joy to the Father's heart as the psalmist reveals when he says, "the Lord takes pleasure in those who fear Him" (Psalm 147:11).

Recently my spouse, Susan, and I were in a department store in one of our favorite shopping malls. As we were picking out a few items I noticed a small security video camera mounted high on a wall and pointed in my direction. I mentioned it to the sales attendant and asked if we were being watched or if we were on television! He chuckled and replied, "Oh, it is not real but just the fact that people think they are being observed in what they are doing is a deterrent to theft and crime." God's camera is everywhere you go. "His eyes are upon everyone observing the good and the bad." If you are conscious of this it will bring a healthy "fear" that will keep you from trouble and disgrace. How is it that fallen preachers have become an epidemic in our generation? Could it be that the church has lost something? Could it be that we are not "walking in the fear of the Lord" as did so many of those who went before us? The question for us is not simply a why question but a what question. The fear of the Lord is a conscious awareness that God is watching and that we can only approach him in reverence and awe, not so much for what He has done, but for who He is.

Chapter Thirteen

A How Question

How can we "walk in the fear of the Lord" in the midst of a "no fear" culture which has not only infiltrated our society but so many of our churches? We begin with the one who has been given the responsibility of leading the only group in the world who lives with a cultural mandate from the One who created it all and who is controlling it all. We begin with the leadership of the local New Testament church. When the church of the Lord Jesus Christ has a healthy concept of the fear of the Lord, it then becomes "salt and light" to its community. Then "walking in the fear of the Lord" we, like the Jerusalem church, will be "multiplied" and will begin to engage our culture and raise high the standard of righteousness which is the only thing that truly exalts a nation.

In order to maintain a wholesome and healthy "fear of the Lord" we must recapture the concept of the seriousness of sin. We are not too serious about it. Tolerance is not only the buzz word for our secular society but for many churches as well. Many simply ignore the seriousness of sin. Some simply laugh it off as if it is simply one of their small vices. Others excuse it by insisting that everyone is doing it and it is just a part of living in a twenty-first century world. Still others minimize it by convincing themselves that it is not as bad as some are doing. But God said he would destroy man because of sin. Yes, he waits with great mercy and patience for the sinner to repent, but if he does not he will ultimately destroy the sin and the sinner with it. He is serious about our sin, so serious He sent his son to a Roman cross. Satan is at work in our world to destroy everyone. When we live with no fear of God we play right into Satan's hands.

So, where do we begin to recover this vital concept of "walking in the fear of the Lord?" We begin with the word of God. Before entering the land of promise God instructed Moses to gather the people and read to them from the law "that they may hear and that they may learn to fear the Lord...and that their children who have not known it, may learn to hear and fear the Lord your God as long as you live in the land which you cross the Jordan to possess" (Deuteronomy 31:10-13). Our spiritual ancestors made their conquest of the land by learning to "walk in the fear of the Lord" and they learned it through the hearing of God's word. The major reason "walking in the fear of the Lord" is a lost concept in the modern church is because exposition of the Word is not a high priority. Many modern church growth gurus are forecasting that sermons of the twenty-first century church will be no more than fifteen minutes in length to accommodate attention spans of biblically illiterate hearers and will be entirely topical in nature. Thus, we will raise another generation who knows little of the word of God, much less the seriousness of sin. The fear of the Lord is imbedded in us only by the planting of the Word in our hearts.

How do we learn to fear the Lord? By hiding the word of God in our hearts. Moses recounts how God instructed him to "gather the people unto Me and, and I will let them hear my words, that they may learn to fear me" (Deuteronomy 4:10). God desires that his people hear his words. Why? So that they may learn to fear him! The primary reason the church lives with so little fear of God today is because of a dangerous void of doctrinal truth emanating from the modern pulpit. Few pulpits truly lift up the awesome majesty of the Lord Jesus Christ before the people.

"Walking in the fear of the Lord" is a choice. Solomon tells of people who "did not choose the fear of the Lord"(Proverbs 1:20-29). It is a choice. We must make a decision to fear Him. The word of God always brings us to a crisis decision, a choice between right and wrong, good and evil.

When I was in high school my dad always wanted to know where I was, what I was doing, and with whom I was doing it! Although I did not admit it at the time I was really glad he cared. My parents made a lot of personal sacrifices for me, one of which was the acquisition of my '56 Chevrolet. The fact that the year was 1965 did not really matter to me. I was so proud of that old car. Unlike a lot of my friends, I had a curfew. On a given night I was gathered with my friends at the local drive-in restaurant and had forgotten about the time which was an hour after I had been instructed to be home. Into the parking lot drove my dad and without saying a word he simply pointed in the direction of home. I got the message, a bit embarrassed at the time in front of my friends. I feared my dad. Oh, not physically. The truth is I could most likely have whipped him at the time. What I really feared was that after all he had sacrificed for me, after all he had done in a thousand ways to show his love for me, I feared that I might disappoint him. As I think about that, I am convinced that this is the kind of fear and reverence that came upon the early church. It was more of a fear of disappointing the One who had given his all for them. Their passion was not so much to be made happy in his sight but to be made holy. For them, "walking in the fear of the Lord" was a conscious choice which came from an abiding love and knowledge of His word.

When we speak of "walking in the fear of the Lord" we are not talking about living with an unhealthy fear of retribution. You will not get very far trying to raise a kid like that. An atmosphere where one dodges in fear of a slap every time he spills the milk is far from the biblical concept. As children of God we should live in the fear that something we do or say might bring dishonor to Him and might disappoint the One who loves us so much that He gave Himself for us.

Balance is the key. There are two extremes at work today which need to be avoided. One extreme develops in the mind an attitude of tolerance and permissiveness so that "anything goes." This extreme makes mockery of God's holiness and judgment. The other extreme overemphasizes the "fire and brimstone" passages and knows little of his tender mercies and loving kindness. This can develop into a psychosis of fear that has no room for compassion and grace. The good news is that God loves us so much that He has provided a way for us to obtain forgiveness. We do not have to suffer for the sins we have committed. The sacrificial, atoning death of the Lord Jesus Christ has covered our sin. Thus we do not live with the fear of God in the sense of being condemned but we do "walk in the fear of the Lord" in the sense of the acknowledgment of his worth and the fear of doing or saying anything that might disappoint or dishonor Him.

The writer of Ecclesiastes sums it up beautifully in the conclusion of his book. "Let us hear the conclusion of the whole matter: *FEAR GOD* and keep His commandments, for this is the whole duty of man." (Ecclesiastes 12:13).

Part Five

Engaging The Culture

I wear glasses because I need them to see. If I take them off, the world is blurred. Why do I wear these glasses? Because they have been prescribed just for me. When I put them on, everything comes into focus. Now, if I put someone else's glasses on, look out. Because when I switch glasses with someone, it's worse than trying to see without lenses. I cannot see anything. Why? Because they were not prescribed for me.

We all look at life through some type of lens. Sometimes we see through glasses that God never intended us to use—glasses of culture, and it's a blur. Some in the church have been looking through no lens at all. Just looking at a world, totally reacting to it, not having a clue about how to engage it. Everything is a blur and out of focus. There is no real definition or directive. We all look at life and culture that is around us through some type of lens. But God gave us some lenses so that when we look at our world, things come into focus.

What is our lens? How do we view the world with focus and clarity? If we only look through the lenses of culture, it's like putting someone else's glasses on. Those lenses can be deceiving. We cannot get clear direction, and sometimes it's worse than no glasses at all.

The lens that God has provided through which we are to view the world is the word of God. When we begin to filter our world around us through this lens of scripture, things that have been blurry, begin to take on definition.

With the lens of the scripture, we are not obsessed that this culture accept us. When we begin to view the world through the lens of scripture, we become consumed with being salt and light to this world. We are able to engage it and ultimately to share our life-changing specs.

Our lens begins taking shape in the first four words of the Bible where we read, "In the beginning God..." What we believe about this statement determines our world view. It determines how we see the world, and how to interpret what is happening in the world around us. I have learned that when I look at the world through the lens of scripture it brings clarity and focus.

Everywhere we turn we see a culture gone awry. Our culture needs a fresh look through our lenses. Everyone seems to be scrambling to address today's social issues. You cannot attend a pastor's conference or any kind of preacher's meeting in this day and age when every speaker is not addressing the culture, wringing their hands, wondering what we are going to do. It's a hot button.

Paul wrote to the Corinthians and told them that what happened to the children of Israel in the wilderness was to set an example. When Joshua's generation came out of those years of wilderness wandering, they knew deprivation. They knew what it was like to be totally dependent on God for their food every day. They knew what it was to need constant direction. They did not know where to go in the wilderness. They understood how to know the presence of God and how to be led by a cloud by day and by a pillar of fire by night.

When they finally came out of the wilderness, within three generations, their children did not know God. We are three generations removed from the great depression and World War II. War and economic ruin brought about the deprivation and dependence on God like Israel's wanderings in the wilderness.

I fear the same pattern is set before us in America. We have a culture that is bringing young people down. What does the church do? Let's be honest. We blame the government, the Supreme Court, and educational systems. But aren't the parents and grandparents entrusted with communicating values to our children? We have a couple of generations of children in America whose parents use television to be their baby-sitters, and parents who try to express their love with material things instead of managed time.

With these methods, can we really expect now to reverse a culture? Do we really care about two generations of young people? Or, are we simply concerned about our own comforts, our own rights, our own cultural preferences?

Saying that we believe in high morals and passing them along to another generation involves more than just passive comments. American culture is buying into God, but I find America is a schizophrenic society. The President comments that he prays for families in Arkansas who lost their children in a shooting. At the inauguration there is Billy Graham, praying. And yet, we do not let a kid pray in a graduation exercise. Talk about a schizophrenic society.

The President of the United States put his hand on the Bible and took the oath of office in front of the whole nation. Administrators in public schools cannot have an open Bible on their desk to counsel a child with biblical truth. We cannot hope that this confused culture will provide corrective lenses for our children.

I could list our social problems on many more pages of this book. The list could even fill a library. Let us ask ourselves why we are not looking at that world through the lens of scripture. How can we engage culture without it? Why is the world a blur? Of course we do not know what to do.

Let's take the first step. Admittedly, many of us are sheltered from this world. All of our connections, all of our fellowship is around our kind. Thus we live and think as if we are still in a world that's governed by an ethic and a culture that is compatible and compassionate with the truth of the Bible. It's the only world some of us know.

This shelter would be all right if Christ had not given us the commission to engage the world. Go out to eat at a restaurant after church one Sunday and take a look around you. Most of the customers around you will not be dressed up from church. We are in the minority.

You say you are not concerned about the culture. Why do the men wear ties in church? Because it's the culture in which we live. It's a cultural expression. Is it biblical? No, there is nothing in the Bible to tell me I have to wear a tie to preach. It's cultural.

If I were in the African bush, I probably would not wear a tie to a worship service. Those people will walk for an hour or two to come to church on Sunday. They would have three or four thousand people under big old tin tabernacles, and they stay there for four, five, and six hours. Why do we have that order of service? It's a cultural expression. These African believers do not have any printed order of worship form. It's a different culture.

Here is the difficult part. Often, the church cannot determine the difference between what is biblical and what is cultural. Consider this. Are we holding cultural wineskins that worked well in the 40s, 50s and 60s. Are these wineskin methods leaking profusely in a world around us that is much more anti-Christian?

Churches all around us are empty today because they hold on to cultural expressions that do not translate to a modern culture. So they are broken, and what happens? Jesus says, the wine spills out and nobody gets the message.

We are called to witness to a lost world. Do you realize that most church growth today comes from people transferring from another church. Largely, we are just recycling. We are moving believers from church to church. There are not really very many people engaging the unchurched, unreached people beyond our gated communities. Christ did not say, "I came to seek and to save those who are members of some other church." No, he said I came to seek and to save those who are lost, outside among another culture. Follow his story. You will find he taught from the steps outside the temple, not from within.

To engage our culture we need to see two things in 1 Chronicles 12:32. We hear about the men of Issacar. They are one of the lesser tribes of Israel.

Issacar was the fifth son of Jacob and Leah. In verse 32, we learn that they understood the times, and second, they knew what Israel should do. These men of Issacar played an important role at a strategic time in the life of Israel. They supported David when his leadership was very fragile. What did they bring to the table? They understood the times around them and they knew what Israel should do.

In the next verse are the men of Zebulun. They were stout-hearted men. They had courage. Look in verse 35, the Danites—the men of Dan. They could keep battle formation. They were team players. They did not become distracted. They stayed in formation. We must be people who are courageous and team players. In verse 8, we learn that the men of God were trained for battle. All these groups brought different things to the table at a time when David's leadership was fragile, but nobody brought anything more important than the men of Issacar. They understood the times and they knew what Israel should do.

Things have not changed. First, we need discernment in comprehending the culture. The sons of Issacar understood the times. Do we?

Second, we need direction in confronting the culture. Many church futurists miss this part. They say we must speak to the culture. However, our job is to confront the culture with the message of Christ in love just as Paul did on Mars Hill in the midst of another pagan culture. Engaging our twenty-first century western culture will involve these two things of us— an understanding of the times and a knowledge of what we should do!

Chapter Fourteen

Discernment in Comprehending the Culture

How is the church going to engage culture? The first thing it's going to take is discernment in comprehending the culture. We are living in a strange moment in history that is being called post-modernism. We know something is wrong. We just are not putting our finger on it. The men of Issacar could. They understood their times. Times change and the challenge of the church is to understand the times in our generation in which we are called to engage our culture.

We have watched the Western culture dramatically change in my lifetime. Think about the '50s. I was a kid in the '50s. It was a time of stability, optimism, and hope. The Christian world view was still dominant. The post-war era was full of promises for the American people. And then came the '60s. The culture began to change, and the music reflected it. Popular music became more introspective and serious. The music began to say, "The answer, my friend, is blowing in the wind, the answer is blowing in the wind." We did not have any answers. Musicians seemed to be reflecting the need of a culture to fit what Augustine called that God-shaped vacuum.

Then came the '70s. The music started bringing a

skepticism. Billy Joel sang, "Only the good die young." Cynicism and skepticism emerged. Should we be surprised? These kids grew up with Watergate and Roe vs. Wade.

And then came the '80s. A conservative resurgence gave us a brief reprieve. It was like the days of Josiah. The economy reversed and made important gains, the interest rate was cut in half, and the economy upswing brought a demand for instant gratification. As a result, consumer debt went through the ceiling.

In the '90s, the evil empire crashed down and the Cold War ended. The West, and democracy, won.

Over the course of these decades, what happened? Did the church influence the culture? I believe the culture influenced the church. Out of all of this sprang the modern so-called seeker-sensitive movement in the church. There is a part of this movement that says we want to make everyone feel comfortable in the church. In some instances, this idea gave rise to an increasing emphasis on the culture and a decreasing emphasis on biblical revelation. If we give in to this trade, we are not getting new wine, just new wineskins. They are empty. The culture is missing the story of the love of our Lord Jesus Christ.

If we are not careful, we will fit in too easily. We need to prepare our seeker service leaders to look at this world through the lens of Scripture. We know that there is something different about a follower of Jesus Christ. You are not supposed to be able to come out into the world and not even be noticed.

The lenses of scripture require that we talk about some difficult, but life-changing things. What do we do with the Bible and its teachings on holiness, sin, blood atonement, conviction, and judgment? We must teach it. We cannot offer the culture a false Gospel that calls for no real New

Testament discipleship. Our lenses require something more than psychological self-help and entertainment.

Throughout these decades rock music has done a better job in determining the direction of culture than the church of Jesus Christ. Somehow, musicians became more serious about impacting their culture than did the church of Jesus Christ.

I was a teenager in the '60s when the Beatles came to America the first time. You know what their hit song was when they first came? They sang,

> *Help! I need somebody.*
> *When I was younger, so much younger than today,*
> *I never needed anybody's help in any way.*
> *But now those days are gone and I'm not so self-assured.*
> *You know, I find I've changed my mind. I've opened up the door.*
> *Help me if you can.*
> *And now my life is changed in oh so many ways.*
> *My independence seems to vanish into haze.*
> *But every now and then I feel so insecure.*
> *I just know I need something like I've never known before.*
> *Help me if you can.*
> *I'm feeling down, and I do appreciate you being 'round.*
> *Help me get my feet back on the ground.*
> *Won't you please, please, help me!*

The Beatles came to America and youth ministers all over America asked their youth groups to burn their records. They shook their fists in the Beatles' faces. One year later those four guys made their first trip to Asia and met a man name the Maharaja. The rest is history.

I have come to be encouraged by what some Christian music artists are doing. They are crossing over. We judged them at first and threw stones at them. Maybe they are attempting to enter the door to the marketplace, to engage the culture and battle for the minds of those young lives by impacting that culture with the message of Jesus Christ.

You know, we Baptists have been pretty good at understanding the Bible. We need to understand the times and how that relates to the message of Jesus Christ. The Gospel is transcultural. It's for everyone. The church should also be transcultural. Our society is becoming more and more transcultural and diverse.

I am a Christian American who happens to be a Baptist, a Christian who happens to be white. Jesus did not stop being what he was when he engaged the Samaritan woman at a well one day. He was a Jew. He is not asking you or me to love rock music. I cannot. He does not ask us to listen to country-western music. I tried. He is saying if cultures collide, choose him and truth every time. When the church presents the truth of Christ to a culture, the testimony and the power of our witness will be truly felt. In a diverse culture, Christ is the one that brings us into oneness.

Understanding and relating to various cultures are not a new thing. William Carey did it in India two centuries ago; Hudson Taylor in China and thousands of other missionaries over the centuries. America is now an unchurched mission field, a different culture than most of us know, and we are called to engage them. Now, we must have direction in confronting the culture.

The men of Issacar understood the times and they knew what Israel should do. Men and women want direction. In a church where I pastored, we got direction from our mission vision statement. We worked hard on it for months. Like Israel, our men and women wanted to know where they were going to go. Our mission sta*tement clarified our direction.*

The world is filled with all sorts of millennial prognosticators. They study the culture. They do their research, make predictions, sell books, and they fill the young minds of preachers with volumes of information on what to do. Let me give you one example.

In *Preaching* magazine a few months back, there was an article by George Barna. He is the best-selling author of forecasting and a futurist for the church. Every preacher I know has many of George Barna's books. I have personally profited from many of them.

In this edition of *Preaching* he admits the value of the Bible, but in the context of speaking to knowing your audience, he says that scripture references, when used in preaching a sermon, may not have the intended impact on young listeners. Relatively few people between ages 25 and 50 know the books of the Bible. They do not even know the most basic popular scriptural verses. Barna said that if preached carelessly, the Bible in an *illiterate audience may unnecessarily be discouraging and repulsive to those hearers.*

This is from the most prolific writer to young preachers. Now, I know what George Barna was saying, but a lot of those young preachers read this and hear this logic: Since the culture does not know the Bible, it may not be wise to use it in the preaching experience because it may "discourage or repulse the listeners." That means that there are churches today that are great at entertainment, but never bring an exposition of the word of God, much less an exegesis of a passage of scripture. In this setting how is the

Holy Spirit going to convict us of sin? If there is no conviction, there is no conversion. Just a feel-good, pseudo-entertainment-type Christianity. These churches may have great new elastic wineskins, but they are filled with air, not the gospel.

It's not all these modern wineskins that build the church of Jesus Christ. The word is the only thing that brings dynamics and direction. Churches must stand on the word and bring it to a culture in a new wineskin.

My good friend, W.A. Criswell, created some new wineskins in his day as no one else did then or today. He understood the times and he reached his generation by doing things with wineskins nobody had ever done before. His church built bowling alleys and all sorts of things to get people to church. Why? Because he not only understood the times, he knew what Israel should do. First Baptist Church of Dallas was built on this way. The bowling alleys were wineskins. They held the wine and kept it from pouring out because they had elasticity.

The gospel was the message. Do not misunderstand. The church stood on the word; the Pastor put it in new wineskins. He was wise enough to know the difference between engaging culture (and remaining in the word) and being influenced by culture (and only seeking to fit in).

The strength is not in wineskins. It's what is in those skins. God's word is to be honored. Many say we should accommodate our message to appease this lost generation. It should be the other way around. The church can be accused of putting the Gospel on the altar of consumerism, simply trying to get a bunch of customers to "buy our product." There is a difference between lenses of scripture and lenses of cultural expression. If you are questioning your vision go back to scripture.

Put on the glasses that show you the truth. Do not look at the world without any corrective lens at all. Do not look at the world with the wrong prescription. Stop looking at the world through somebody else's glasses.

It's amazing what happens when I put *my* glasses back on. I get clarity. I find definition. We all look at life and our culture through some type of lens. What pair of lenses are you wearing today?

Chapter Fifteen

Direction in Confronting the Culture

The Church of Jesus Christ in the Western world has largely lost two generations of young adults. They have never sung a Christian hymn, never heard the Gospel. Many of them, the children of church members, are lost to Christ and lost to the church. So the church wrings its hands in panic, wondering how we are going to reach them. Some compromise, hoping that by compromising the Gospel message they will make it more palatable for this culture that is foreign to the Gospel.

There was an ABC special a year or two ago where they interviewed a pastor in America and asked him why he did not have a cross on his church. He said to try to capture the essence of Christianity with a single symbol is dangerous. But if Christianity is not about a cross, it does not have a message.

So some of us compromise. Some of us condone. It is amazing how in some churches, Baptist churches, we now condone alternative lifestyles, hoping we will win favor with folks who are outside the church.

Some of us don't compromise and do not condone these lost generations. We condemn. We just beat our Bibles a little harder and scream a little louder and condemn them as though that were going to win them back to the church and back to the Savior.

A few churches have discovered what it is to confront a lost culture through the love of Jesus Christ and through the power of the Gospel.

God has given us a lens through which he intends for us to view the world around us, our own world. The lens is scripture. And one of the problems in the church of the Lord Jesus Christ today is that many people are viewing the world around them only through the lens of culture. In fact, I fear sometimes we have leaned so far over to speak to our culture that some of us in the church have fallen victim to it.

When you begin to look at your world through the word of God, your world becomes defined. Your world comes into focus. You begin to see some things clearly, as never before. That's the purpose of this chapter: that we might understand that God has a lens for us through which to view our world.

The men of Issacar did that. They understood the times and because they looked through that lens they knew what they should do. Francis Schaeffer was a cultural prophet in the highest sense of the word. Many have read his books such as, *How Should We Then Live?,* and other books that he has published. A brilliant theologian and cultural prophet, he ran the L'abri Fellowship in Switzerland for many years. More than 30 years ago Francis Schaeffer predicted that we would pass from a Judeo-Christian culture to a post-Judeo-Christian culture, and Francis Schaeffer lived to see that day. He has been dead for many years, but he would look at our Western world today and rightly exclaim that no longer are we even in a post-Judeo-Christian culture, but we live today in an anti-Judeo-Christian culture.

What has happened in our culture? A few years ago our failures, our personal shortcomings and perversions were occasions of shame and guilt and embarrassment. Today, do you know what they are? They are an occasion to star on the Sally Jessy Rafael show or Jerry Springer or a dozen other shows like that. Why? Because our culture has lost its moorings. It's sick. The things that once slithered down the back alleys of America, now parade proudly right down Main Street before our eyes.

We are a schizophrenic society. We say one thing, we do another. We are a culture that is without moorings: that has lost its roots. Go to the Supreme Court building in Washington, DC, and enter the room where the Supreme Court Justices sit. The Chief Justice sits in the middle. Above his chair carved in granite is a copy of the tablets of the Ten Commandments. Upstairs is the Supreme Court law library. The library is trimmed in mahogany and carved in mahogany on the wall is the Ten Commandments.

But, we read in the newspapers that a judge in Gadsden, Alabama, was ordered to modify or remove a plaque of the Ten Commandments from his court room, a display the governor has promised to defend with force if necessary.

This is the culture we have a commission to reach and engage. It's a post-modern world and many of us are sheltered from what is really happening in that world because all of our connections and all of our fellowship and all of our social interaction is done where we live. Some of us think our culture is still a culture that's compatible with and compassionate toward the truth of God's word. It's not. It's not even a post-Christian world out there. It is a tremendously anti-Christian world out there.

Christ gave us a command to take the Gospel to every person. He gave us a command to get outside the walls of our churches and present the Gospel of Jesus Christ to every person. The church exploded in Acts when Paul and others stepped out of their comfort zones and engaged a culture similar to ours. You talk about an anti-Christian culture; theirs certainly was far more so than ours. You talk about a pagan culture, the one Paul reached was just that. We must employ every means within scriptural confinements to engage them. Just as our missionaries have taken the Gospel message and applied it cross-culturally for decades, the church of Jesus Christ has to take on a missionary mentality because this is a mission field around us. We live in a culture that knows nothing of the Savior that we hold dear to our hearts.

Now, we cannot sit here and expect that culture to come to us. They are not going to do it. Many of us were brought up in a Judeo-Christian culture. I have vivid memories of prayer in public schools in Fort Worth. I remember the Ten Commandments on the wall in Miss Pool's class room. I remember daily Bible readings. I remember when the church was the most respected and esteemed institution in the city.

Some of us have been in church every week for 30 years and many of our contacts are restricted to the church. It's easy for us to think that *our* world is who we're trying to reach, but it's not. The world out there we are called to engage is one that is a different culture from what most of us know anything about.

And so, here we are to engage our culture, what is it going to take? The answer is found in 1 Chronicles 12:32.

First, it's going to take discernment in comprehending this culture. How are we going to reach a culture around us if we know nothing about them? How are you going to go to a mission field where the Gospel has never been and reach that culture if you do not learn everything you can about that culture? The church of Jesus Christ knows very little about the culture that's around us today.

The men of Issacar understood the times in which they lived. It's going to take discernment in comprehending our culture. Jesus was often confronted with those who were clinging to old wineskins, and when he did, he said something to them in Matthew 16:3. In his rebuke of those Pharisees, he said "you cannot discern the signs of the times, you don't even know what's going on around you. You don't even know the times around you." I wonder if Jesus Christ came back to the church of Christ today all over the Western world, if he wouldn't be saying to us, "You don't even understand the signs of the times around you."

Second, we need direction in confronting our culture. The men of Issacar understood the times and they knew what Israel should do. It's one thing to understand the times, and it seems like that's what most of us in church growth circles today are consumed with. But where I believe so many of us are missing it, from a New Testament biblical pattern, is that many of us still do not know what the church should do.

We do not have direction in confronting the culture, and the reason we do not is because many of us in the church have been looking for direction everywhere except in our own manual. We have been looking at this culture through the lens of culture itself, and we have gotten blurred vision. We do not know what we should do.

We live in a fast-fix, how-to world. Why should we cook from scratch today when you can put it in the microwave for 30 seconds? That's the world we live in. I was thumbing through a video tape catalogue when I saw: *How to have a happy marriage in five easy lessons.* Think about that. Must have been a Catholic priest. No one can have a happy marriage in five easy lessons. It takes work.

We live in such a fast-fix microwave world that it's now spilled over into our pulpit. What we want to do is just tell people how to do this, how to do that. Here are three easy lessons to go out and do without any call of picking up a cross, without any call of New Testament discipleship.

We are told in preaching conferences literally to keep it light and informal, with humor and filled with personal anecdotes. If you listen to a lot of modern preaching professors today, you get the idea that Jesus Christ was just a self-help therapist who went around helping people feel good about themselves. That's not the Christ of the Bible.

Is this the church that Christ and the Apostles built? Look at Simon Peter's first recorded sermon at Pentecost in Acts 2. Read Paul's first recorded sermon in Acts 13. Look at the pattern. Paul was not in Jerusalem. He was in Antioch. Peter was in Jerusalem in chapter 2, but to whom was he preaching? He was preaching to people from all over the world that had come there for Pentecost. Cross-culturally.

When he spoke to them the message in Acts 2, he preached Christ crucified, buried, risen and coming again. He said to his hearers, "You, with the help of wicked individuals, have nailed him to a cross." The sermons in the New Testament were culturally relevant but they were power-packed.

What is the common denominator in New Testament preaching when we see these preachers? They were preaching out there in a culture that was foreign to the one they knew. A pagan, godless culture like ours. The common denominator is their *dependence upon the Holy Spirit and apostolic revelation.* The word of God: Bible preaching was centered in the person of Jesus Christ. Every one of those messages was sin-exposing, self-convicting, life-challenging. This is in direct opposition to much of the light, informal and Christianized self-help entertainment that's prevalent today.

What happened when these apostles preached in those foreign cultures? The Bible says when they heard Peter preach their hearts were cut. We have a word for that. It's called conviction. Conviction. When they preached in the power of God's Spirit, God spoke to the people's hearts. He spoke to them the word of God and the prophet said the word was like a hammer that breaks a rock to pieces and conviction came into their hearts, and they said, *What shall we do*? They did not know what to do. They said *What shall we do,* and the answer was, *Change your mind, repent.* Their obedience resulted in thousands being swept into the Kingdom of God.

Pastors are getting plenty of counsel these days about how and what to preach. Here's a quotation from a famous minister who said: Preachers "who pick out texts from the Bible and then proceed to give the historical settings and the primary meanings in the context are grossly misusing the Bible. Could any procedure be more surely predestined to dullness and futility? One out of a hundred people in your congregation doesn't care what Moses or Isaiah or Paul or John meant in those verses spoken 2000 years ago. Let the sermon start with thinking about the hearer's needs, and then let the whole sermon be organized around the constructive endeavor to meet those felt needs. This is good sense and good psychology."

This is what we are hearing today. But, this quotation is more than 50 years old from Harry Emerson Fosdick, the most liberal preacher "theologian" of the first half of the 20th century. Fifty years ago this theological liberal counseled his generation the same way that some modern *conservative* evangelicals are being counseled today. It is the same philosophy. It did not work then and it will not work now. The people that bought into it were those mainline denominations that put the Bible aside and followed this philosophy of Fosdick. Today these churches and denominations are dead, dying or shriveling up.

The tension we feel today is the same as they felt in the first century. We are in the world but not of the world. Compromise may be the best description of the church of the '90s. The world seems to set our agenda. We once gave primary importance to knowing the Bible. Now you go to preaching conferences and young preachers are taught to know the audience first.

Today there are all kinds of new networks of churches springing up, but they are centered on methodology, not on the gospel. Acts 2:42, for example, continuing in the apostle's doctrine and fellowship and breaking bread and prayer, is no longer the pattern for the modern church. Today we are told that to attract unbelievers we must meet their felt needs, and help them feel better about themselves and our message. That's fine, but that is not what the church is to do, according to Acts 2.

We become so obsessed with trying to relate to the culture in a contemporary world and wanting them to like us and wanting them to be attracted to us, that we fall into the culture ourselves, and compromise the very dynamic and power that we have at our disposal to engage them— The word of the living God.

The Bible is not trying to speak to the modern world. It is seeking to convert it. The Gospel is a culture unto itself. You cannot learn to speak French by reading an English translation of Victor Hugo's *Les Miserables*. You have to go to the language. You have to look at the syntax. You have to learn the vocabulary. Men and women are never going to know about Christianity by having it translated into the language of self-help. What many are doing when we say we are speaking to the culture is merely adapting it instead of presenting the Gospel to it.

What is the Gospel? The Bible says the Gospel is the Good News that Jesus suffered and died on a cross, took your sin in his own body so you could take his righteousness. Died your death so you could live his life. He was buried and three days later he arose from the grave, and today he is the living Lord and Savior who can forgive your sins and come into your life and give you purpose and peace. Now that's the Good News.

The church today has largely lost a couple of generations. These groups of people are known by several names: Generation X, Baby Busters, etc. Their groups have distinct characteristics, but my research has shown there are five characteristics with which they can be identified.

If you want to understand the times here are five thoughts on the minds of these young adults.

First, they are searching for meaningful relationships in life. More than anything else that's what they want. Many of them have never known a meaningful relationship. They are a young generation that are products of massive divorce, and many of them are homesick for a home they never had. They want someone with whom they can interact, with whom they can connect, somebody who will care. That is the primary thirst of their heart.

A second characteristic about them is they want immediate gratification. They do not want to wait for anything. Give it to me but give it to me right now, they say. They want to get in the stock market and get a return tomorrow. It's a part of the culture in which they have been raised. They want popcorn, they put it in the microwave and have it in a few seconds.

The third characteristic is that they want something for nothing. Give it to me, they say, but give it to me without cost or condition. Many of them have never had to work for anything in life. Everything was given to them. They develop the mentality that they expect something and they want it for nothing.

The fourth characteristic is they are searching for guilt-free living, and the irony is, 81 percent of them, don't even believe in absolute truth. Yet, at night when they turn the light off in their room, they want guilt-free living. Though they do not articulate it, they want forgiveness.

The fifth characteristic is they are searching for prosperity and do not have much hope of obtaining it. This is the first generation in American history that will probably raise their kids in homes that are not as nice as the ones in which they were raised. They think they have gotten a bum deal. Their moms and dads grew up in the '60s in a time of free love. They grew up in the time of AIDS. They think they are getting a bum deal. Their mom and dad grew up in a time when they got out of school and went into high-level entry jobs and had plenty of opportunity for advancement. Many of them got out of school a few years ago in a time of down-sizing and they are thirsty for a prosperity they do not have much hope of obtaining.

What is the first thing that this generation wants? They are searching for meaningful relationships in life, but we are offering them coffee and doughnuts.

These young adults want immediate gratification. The church says our services are less than an hour and you will have plenty of time to enjoy the rest of the day.

They want something for nothing. They do not want to pay for anything. We say come to our church and when you do, leave your wallet at home. Can you imagine Jesus who taught so much about stewardship saying come to worship me but leave your wallet at home? Do you see what churches are trying to do? They know what this generation needs. They understand the times, but they do not know what Israel should do. We think what Israel should do is go out there and meet them and *appease them on their terms*.

These lost generations to the church want guilt-free living, so what does the church tell them? You can come to our church and blend in with the crowd and nobody will notice and you can "remain anonymous as long as you like." In other words, there is nothing different between us and you. Come and you can just blend in with everybody else.

They are thirsty for prosperity, do not have much hope of obtaining it, and that's why the church has a prosperity Gospel. Do we know what Israel should do? We are the only ones that have the answer. The lens through which we are to see our world is the word of God.

Let's just pretend the Bible is a computer, and type into that computer the word PURPOSE. If you boil all five of those common characteristics of the lost generations down, it comes to one word, purpose. We are looking for purpose in life. And now begin to narrow the search, you will narrow the search to the New Testament.

Click that little mouse again and narrow the search another time and you will come to the Epistles. Click it again and you'll come to the Epistle to the Ephesians. Narrow the search one more time and you will come to Ephesians 1. Narrow the search one final time and you will come to one verse in this Bible that has the answer to all five needs of that lost generation, and which will give us direction in confronting the culture: Ephesians 1:7. "In Him we have redemption through His blood, the forgiveness of sins, according to the riches of His grace."

The first characteristic of this lost generation is that they are searching for meaningful relationships in life. In Eph. 1:7: "In him we have redemption." In Him. They don't know that what we are about is a relationship. They think the church is about religion. They think the church is living in an out-of-date world, that we are not relevant to anything. They do not know that what we are about is a personal relationship.

You only have three relationships in life:

The outward expression, which is your relationship with others. This is the relationship where you connect with those in interpersonal relationships—your wife, your husband, your kids, your mom, your dad, your church friends, your friends in the social arena or on the golf course—we have relationships with one another. We have a relationship with our family and with our friends, an outward expression where we connect with them. Life is about relationships.

We have a second relationship that's an inward expression. A relationship with yourself that largely has been perverted in many Christian circles today. When I awake every morning and shave and look at myself, I have a relationship with myself. I live with myself. Much of what happens in my relationship with my wife Susie, or my friends, when it's not right, it's simply a projection of what's really going on inside me.

We have the capacity for an upward expression. This is what distinguishes us from all the other created order. To come into relationship with God through Jesus Christ is unique to us. We have the privilege to begin to know him in the intimacy of Father and Son in a vital, living relationship.

The bottom line is, you are never properly related to others until you are properly related to yourself, and you are never properly related to yourself until you come into relationship with God through Jesus Christ and realize how indescribably valuable you are to him.

When you come to know Christ in a relationship, you begin to find your self-worth, not in five easy steps, but in the person of Jesus Christ, you begin to touch other people's lives. Then, you have true, lasting relationships. We are the only ones that have the answer, if we know what Israel should do.

The lost generation wants immediate gratification. They do not want to wait for anything. Look at the next phrase in Ephesians. 1:7: "In Him *we have* redemption." Right now, occurring in actual time. We do not have to wait for it. You know what the world thinks? They think what we are about is pie in the sky by and by. They do not know that what we have to offer them is for right now. We have redemption. Now, we are not just about an eternal life, but an abundant, joyful, purposeful life right now.

This generation wants something for nothing. Look at the next phrase. "In Him we have redemption through his blood." They do not know that Jesus Christ has already paid for their abundant life, that it's purchased for them already with His blood. The very thing they want, something for nothing, is the gift that God has to give them. But they do not know it because we've been out there trying to make them feel good about themselves. We have never translated it for them. You know what they think? They think Jesus went to a cross and shed His blood and made a down payment and they have to work and earn their way and be as good as they can to make it to heaven. They do not know that when He went to a cross, He paid their sin debt in full.

It's finished. He did it all. He is the answer to their very hearts' need.

This generation wants guilt-free living. We are the only ones who have the answer. In him we have redemption through his blood, *the forgiveness of sins.* They are not going to find guilt-free living by being able to blend in with everybody else so they will be anonymous. Blending in and becoming anonymous does not take care of the need of the human heart.

Do you know that guilt is not your foe? I mean authentic guilt. There is a lot of artificial guilt today heaped on people by others through abuse and other events that lead people to have guilt that is not theirs to bear. That's all artificial. But I am talking about authentic guilt. It's not your foe, it's your friend. Often, guilt is God's way of saying, "You have sinned."

What is confession, *homolegeo?* It means to say the same as, to agree with God. So, guilt is God's way of saying you have sinned. Confession is just our way of saying, God, I agree with you. The forgiveness of sins is what this world is looking for, but they are not finding guilt-free living out there in the corrupt culture. We are the only ones who have the answer, but most of us hold our peace. And others of us look so far into the culture, compromising and condoning it that people can blend into our church and not be any different from those who are already there.

The very thing for which they are looking is forgiveness of sins. Only Jesus Christ can grant eternal forgiveness. That's the Good News of this relationship with Him for which they are searching.

Finally, they are thirsty for prosperity. They do not think they are ever going to get it. The last phrase is where prosperity is really to be found. "In Him we have redemption through His blood, forgiveness of sins according to the riches of His grace." Here's the way Paul put it. "For you know the grace of our Lord Jesus Christ, that though He was rich, for your sakes became poor that you, through His poverty, might become rich." (2 Corinthians 8:9).

I am glad that when Ephesians 1:7 was written down, Paul used a preposition *according to* rather than *out of*. There is a big difference in these riches *being out* of the riches of his grace and *according to* the riches of his grace.

If I took a one dollar bill out of my wallet and gave it to you, I would be giving "out of my riches." If I took a blank check and wrote down O.S. Hawkins on the bottom of it and gave it to you and said do what you want to with it, then I have given "according to my riches."

Look what you have in Christ. "In him we have redemption through his blood, the forgiveness of sins, according to the riches of his grace." It's the very thing for which this lost generation is looking. We are the only ones who have the answer.

I remember vividly the first time that I ever saw the word *redemption*. When I was almost eight years old, I really wanted a ball glove. I saw in a catalog that for two-and-a-half books of S&H Green Stamps I could get a genuine leather ball glove. I went through weeks of my mom letting me have her grocery stamps. I would stick those stamps in those books, and finally after a few months I had enough books to get a genuine leather ball glove. One Saturday my Dad drove me to the south side of Fort Worth, where we stopped in a parking lot beside a big white concrete block building. I saw a word I had never seen in my life. It's in Ephesians 1:7. Redemption. I had never heard of that word, never seen it before, did not know what it meant. I remember walking in that store looking at it: S&H Green

Stamp Redemption Center. I went in with my catalogue and books of green stamps and gave them to the woman behind the counter. She thumbed through every page. My heart started fluttering. What if I forgot a page? She went through all of them and disappeared into the back room. Minutes later, seemed like hours, she came out and with a box. She put it on the counter and I opened it. Inside was a genuine leather baseball glove.

I put it on my hand and started patting the pocket. I kept it on all the way home. Some teenager up the street said I should put some linseed oil in the pocket, wrap a ball inside and tie it off with a rubber band at night. I slept with that glove for three weeks. I redeemed that glove with two-and-a-half books of S&H Green Stamps.

And so our Lord one day went to redemption's counter for you. His Father sent him. Down he came, past the solar systems and constellations and through measureless space, down still farther—think about it—to be planted as a seed in the womb of a young virgin girl, to be that helpless. To gestate in that womb. Then to be born in the dung and filth of a Bethlehem stable. Then down still farther, to go about doing good and being beaten and mocked and spit on and have his beard plucked out with our hands, and finally to walk up to redemption's counter and put down his own blood. Why? So he could take you home with him. That is still the message of the Gospel. In him we have redemption through his blood, the forgiveness of sins according to the riches of his grace.

We are the only ones who have the answer, but some of us have looked into this culture and studied it so long, we have fallen into it. Some of us have forgotten the true *Seeker*, the one with the capital S, and it's time that some of us take off the lens of culture, put on the lens of scripture, and confront the lost generation with the loving Gospel of the Lord Jesus Christ:

We must needs go home by the way of the cross. *There's no other way but this.* We shall ne'er get sight of the gates of light if the way of the cross we miss. The way of the cross leads home and it's sweet to know as we onward go the way of the cross leads home.

In Him we have redemption, through His blood, the forgiveness of sins according to the riches of His grace.

So here are my glasses. I look at my world without them, and I see confusion. It's just a blur, without definition, without direction. I take someone else's glasses that are handed to me and I put them on, and it's just as bad or worse. Many people are going through life looking at their world with glasses someone else gave them, and they are not their prescription. God has a prescription for us, and as we put them on, just as I put my prescription glasses on, things come into focus. We begin to see things clearly. When you begin to look at your life through the lens of one who loved you so much that he gave himself for you, your life will take on clarity. Your life will take on focus. And you will begin to see clearly a world around us we are called to reach.

What will it be for the Twenty-First Century Church—SHIELDS OF BRASS OR SHIELDS OF GOLD?